farmhouse vegetables

a vegetable-forward cookbook

michael smith

PENGUIN
an imprint of Penguin Canada, a division of Penguin Random House Canada Limited

Canada • USA • UK • Ireland • Australia • New Zealand • India • South Africa • China

First published 2023

www.penguinrandomhouse.ca

Library and Archives Canada Cataloguing in Publication

Title: Farmhouse vegetables : a vegetable-forward cookbook / Michael Smith.
Names: Smith, Michael, 1966 October 13- author.
Description: Includes index.
Identifiers: Canadiana (print) 20220407738 | Canadiana (ebook) 20220407746 | ISBN 9780735242241 (hardcover) | ISBN 9780735242258 (EPUB)
Subjects: LCSH: Cooking (Vegetables) | LCSH: Vegetarian cooking. | LCGFT: Cookbooks.
Classification: LCC TX801 .S62 2023 | DDC 641.6/5—dc23

Cover and book design: Matthew Flute
Cover and interior photography: Al Douglas
Food Media Producer: Nghe Tran

Printed and bound in China

10 9 8 7 6 5 4 3 2 1

For Jason, a cook, friend, fellow forager, and farmer.
Jason is back in our kitchen after his accident . . . to all our vegetables together.

contents

1 introduction
5 the making of a farm
7 our culinary farm
8 farmer kevin
11 sustainable, regenerative agriculture
12 new old-fashioned farming
15 our prince edward island terroir
16 today's farm project
19 life-cycle harvesting
20 seeds, the seed house, and the sprout house
23 the herb house and herb garden
24 the mushroom patch project
27 happy animals
28 trial garden

farmhouse vegetarian

33 **sorrel hummus**
sourdough crackers, sumac chili oil
34 **vegetable broth and vegetable tea**
37 **shiitake gai lan noodle bowl**
umami broth, enoki nori tarragon tangle
38 **radish, smashed cucumber, tofu, and hemp heart salad**
borage flowers, salad burnet, garden tangle, preserved lemon dressing
41 **tomatoes, nasturtiums, and golden halloumi**
honey dressing
43 **shiitake cabbage tacos**
green lentil smear, green jam
45 **beets, fire grains, and fresh ricotta with rosemary**
49 **lentil soup**
pea and mint fritters, lentil sprouts
51 **kabocha squash and ancho cider broth**
sage, pumpkin seed, and goat cheese pesto, spicy roasted chickpeas
54 **baked tomatoes, fennel, garlic, and feta**
orecchiette, wilted spinach

57 **asparagus dill frittata**
shaved asparagus salad

59 **cauliflower mac 'n' cheese**
avonlea cheddar, caraway rye crust

60 **quinoa feta stuffed bell peppers**
yellow tomato sauce

63 **soba noodle bowl with golden tofu, garden peas, cinnamon basil, miso carrot broth**

64 **bok choy and edamame**
ginger lime coconut broth, sweet potato jasmine rice

67 **mujadara and wilted kale**
cumin browned onions, preserved lemon dressing

farmhouse vegetables

70 **root vegetable pavé**
rosemary beet purée, roast garlic labneh

75 **root vegetable chowder**
whey, cream, butter

76 **whole roasted celery root**
celery lovage slaw, lovage oil

79 **whole roasted turnip**
cranberry rosemary chutney

80 **roasted beets**
mint labneh

83 **grilled carrots**
carrot horseradish jam

84 **grilled parsnips**
parsley chimichurri

87 **potato turnip mash**
rosemary maple brown butter

88 **cracked potatoes**
sage brown butter

91 **potato gnocchi, nutmeg spinach sauce, and orach salad**

93 **cumin corn fritters, fresh pea mash, and purslane**
ancho squeeze

97 **fried sunchokes**
mushroom ketchup

98 **cider-braised baby leeks**
warm apple vinaigrette, crispy leeks

101 **whole roasted onions, grilled garlic scapes, and chive flowers**
nutmeg soubise, crispy shallots

105 **many peas and mint salad**
minted pea purée

106 **mushy green beans and tarragon**
carrot almond butter, crispy onions

109 **greens, herbs, and flowers**
farmhouse dressing

110 **confit tomato, poblano, and garlic**

113 **grilled zucchini**
green coriander seed salsa

114 **grilled summer squash**
grilled corn poblano relish

117 **basil ratatouille and swiss chard wraps**
tomato marigold salsa

119 **lion's mane mushroom steaks**
brown butter béarnaise sauce

123 **grilled eggplant baba ganoush**
za'atar-spiced eggplant chips

124 **fennel marmalade**

127 **fennel mustard pickle slaw**

128 **fresh ice plant salsa**

131 **cauliflower chickpea fritters**
broccoli garlic sauce

132 **grilled broccolini**
oyster garlic glaze

135 **roasted brussels sprouts, bean sprouts, broccoli sprouts, and cashews**
kimchi miso dressing

136 **whole roasted cauliflower**
ancho cider poached, spiced brown butter hollandaise

139 **cauliflower steaks**
horseradish cauliflower cream

140 **wilted cabbage**
tarragon, cream

143 **roasted butternut squash steaks**
sage, pumpkin seed, and goat cheese pesto

144 **maple-spiced sweet potato**
cilantro cashew pesto

147 **honey-roasted sunflower head**

vegetables and meat

151 cucumber radish salad with tarragon tonnato
radish sprouts

152 chef nghe tran's goi ga (vietnamese cabbage chicken slaw)

155 bacon-steamed baby turnips and greens

156 smoked salmon celery root brandade
caraway rye crackers

159 corn and smoked salmon chowder
grilled corn basil relish

160 broccoli clam chowder
garlic thyme broth, cracker crumbs

163 potatoes and beef
baked potatoes and cracklings, beefy roast potatoes

164 bacon, baked beans, and kale

167 potato, leek, mushroom, and chicken skillet stew

168 slow-roasted pork, poblano, fennel, and tomatoes
fennel frond dressing

171 grilled summer salad
lemon garlic yogurt dressing, miso turnip purée

meat and vegetables

175 potato-crusted smoked salmon cakes
arugula dill salad, maritime mustard pickles

177 beefy vegetable stew
farmhouse beef broth

181 roast eggplant-wrapped salmon
tomato garlic mash

182 root vegetable and roast chicken pan stew

185 melted cabbage, turnip, and ham hock

186 slow-roasted duck and winter vegetables
rosemary roasted applesauce

189 pan-roasted cauliflower, leek, apple, and cinnamon-crusted pork tenderloin

farmhouse sips and treats

193 tomato lillet splash
marigold ice cubes

194 herb house lemonade
lemon verbena, lemon balm, lemon thyme, local moonshine

197 cucumber gin ice pops
borage blossom confetti

198 "anne's mistake" raspberry cordial

201 ice cream sandwiches
carrot cake cookies, parsnip ice cream

203 strawberry rhubarb pavlova
lavender cream

207 jalapeño chocolate chip cookies

208 old-school rhubarb
tarragon sugar

211 sweet corn fritters
tarragon blueberry stew, maple crème fraîche

212 butternut squash pie
pumpkin seed crust, bourbon cream

215 winter squash thyme skillet cake
rosemary vanilla cream

farmhouse pantry

218 maritime mustard pickles
219 red chili flakes
220 sesame za'atar
220 preserved lemon dressing
221 preserved lemon purée
222 lentil sprouts
222 pickled red onions
223 farmhouse chicken broth
224 farmhouse yogurt
225 farmhouse crème fraîche
225 fresh ricotta with rosemary

229 special ingredients, farm resources, and contacts
231 my special thanks
235 index

introduction

I love vegetables, everything about them. I'm amazed by their diversity, inspired by their flavours, and impressed by their nutritive value. As a farmer I love the intricate challenges of growing vegetables sustainably. As a teacher I'm thankful for the knowledge we harvest far beyond the crop. As a chef I'm inspired by the creative potential of our culinary farm. As a passionate cook I enjoy the artful simplicity and infinite methodology of cooking them. Above all else, I love how I feel when I eat a whole lot of vegetables.

I love meat too, but I eat less of it these days, preferring the limited production of small family farms to mass quantities from distant, ethically dubious operations. My family regularly derives protein from plants, just as animals do, and we often enjoy the vegetables that accompany the meat more than the meat itself. We're omnivores, with a healthy, balanced diet of minimal meat and maximum vegetables.

At the Inn at Bay Fortune our culinary farm provides our kitchen with impeccable vegetables for our guests and a lifetime of learning for our team. The rhythms and rituals of our culinary farm simultaneously connect us to time immemorial while keeping us grounded in the day-to-day moments that make life so special. The best path in your life is to just eat as many fruits and vegetables as you can along the way. You'll have all the bright energy you need to learn as you go.

I learned healthy cooking from my mom, then forgot when I learned how to cook in a restaurant. I learned again for my family and once again for our guests at the Inn at Bay Fortune. I know now that cooking is an expression of life itself, and that vegetables are the key ingredient. As a cook I discovered the better they taste, the more you eat. As a dad I learned the better they taste, the better they are for you. As a farmer I learned the better they taste, the better they are for the environment.

Cook like a farmer, with the seasons as your guide and bounty your patient reward. Celebrate diversity, try as many different types of freshly grown local vegetables as you can get your hands on, and embrace sustainability. Find your favourite flavours and return to them over and over, but never stop trying new things.

In this cookbook you'll find the ingredients, techniques, and ideas you need to fully develop your own vegetable cooking style. You'll find lots of ways to continue enjoying meat (or not) on your terms while making vegetables (and lots of fruits) your first choice in the kitchen.

The Vegetable-Meat Spectrum

There are many healthy approaches to what we eat, each valid in its own way, all valuing ethically sourced ingredients. Some of us eat everything under the sun, some focus on vegetables with or without dairy and eggs, some avoid certain meats, others eat fish but not meat. Regardless of our preferences, we all need protein to survive and can easily find it in a plant-based diet. Simply put, we thrive when we eat lots of vegetables.

Choose your stance, from intensely vegan to ravenously carnivorous, then realign your perspective. This conversation is not about removing meat from our cooking. The strategy is even simpler: just put vegetables first.

Meat and Vegetables: A traditional North American view of the plate, more meat than vegetables, often the same meats in rotation, thus missing diversity, with lots of potatoes but other healthy vegetables missing or relegated to occasional side dishes and salads.

Vegetables and Meat: A contemporary approach aligned with global trends, emphasizing healthy fruits and vegetables as the centrepiece of the meal with meat as a secondary component or flavourful condiment. The environmentally conscious choice.

Vegetarian and Vegan: An excellent way to fully enjoy the bright, vibrant benefits of fruits, vegetables, grains, and legumes while proving that humans can more than survive without meat—we can thrive.

Inside This Book

This collection of recipes reflects all that I've learned about vegetable cookery and the incredible variety of our culinary farm. You'll find the dishes organized into the following chapters. From full vegetarian meals to simple side dishes, as well as cocktails and desserts, there's always a place at the table for vegetables.

Farmhouse Vegetarian: Multi-component fully vegetarian meals, some lacto-ovo, some vegan, emphasizing the full flavour of vegetables, with grains, legumes, nuts, seeds, and plant-based and dairy protein sources.

Farmhouse Vegetables: Centrepiece main dishes and spectacular side dishes showcasing a particular vegetable or part of the farm. These dishes easily fit into a vegetarian diet but don't include plant-based protein.

Vegetables and Meat: Vegetable-forward dishes that include meat as a condiment, secondary component, or just a simple way to add distinctive rich flavour without corresponding heaviness.

Meat and Vegetables: These farmhouse suppers are inspired by traditional more-meat-than-veg dishes. I've updated them by simply adding lots more vegetables to the basic mix. They're full meals, hearty but not heavy.

Farmhouse Sips and Treats: Vegetables offer as much creative potential behind our farm bar as they do in the savoury kitchen. They're at home in the pastry kitchen too, where impeccable freshness, natural sweetness, and distinctive flavours are always a part of the mix. We love the creative challenge!

Farmhouse Pantry: Recipes for essential basics and creative condiments to keep your pantry well stocked with homemade flavours preserved for another day.

Recipe and Kitchen Notes

Use Lots: On a farm it's often all or nothing. Months pass waiting to harvest a particular vegetable, then one day we're overrun with bounty. We learn to let the harvest guide the menu, and when a particular ingredient is at its peak, we extravagantly show it off.

Use More, Use Less: Successful cooking is as much a function of exact precision as loose flexibility. Vegetables vary, plans change, go with the flow. Use more of something if you like, or less, or substitute as need be.

Yields: Most of the recipes in this book serve an average family of four to six people. Many dishes can be portioned as a main course for a few or a side dish for many. Combine several of your favourites to enjoy a full, satisfying plant-based meal.

Tools and Techniques: Embrace modern digital technology to accurately gauge time and temperature. Invest in high-quality, heavy-duty cookware, care for it, and reap the rewards for a lifetime. Read through the full recipe before diving in, so you know what to expect, and take the time to do all the suggested prep before starting to cook.

Substitute Ingredients: A number of the ingredients in these recipes are unique to our farm or to Prince Edward Island. Some are foraged wild. For the more obscure ingredients, whenever possible I've suggested a substitution. Your results won't be the same, of course, but they will be delicious in their own way. In some cases there just aren't any viable options. If you're interested in tracking down the real thing, you'll find lots of information on page 229.

Animal Fats: One of the hallmarks of our style of plant-based cooking is the judicious use of animal fats. Like any good kitchen we prefer not to waste resources, so we carefully save the various fats that come our way, mainly pork, beef, chicken, and duck. A few drops in a vegetable dish can add lots of deliciousness without the heaviness of the meat itself. At home we'll often enjoy an entire meatless meal except for a bit of animal fat in one dish. Of course, these are optional ingredients and our vegetarian friends can easily omit them.

Doneness: So much of vegetable cookery is simply learning to respect each vegetable as unique, understanding that each reaches a point of perfection when colours have deepened, flavours have emerged, and textures have softened. Once you learn to spot that magical moment, the rest is easy.

Presentation: We all enjoy beautifully presented food, a feast for our eyes before our bellies. As cooks we show respect for our ingredients and our guests by taking the time to make our presentations as beautiful as possible. When you have ready access to a farm or garden, feel free to garnish with reckless abandon!

the
making
of a
farm

our culinary farm

Culinary Farm: a farm devoted to one restaurant kitchen, to growing impeccable produce for its guests while educating its cooks and inspiring their cooking through daily connection to the hard work and joy of sustainable farming.

Over time, our farm has grown to more than eight acres and now includes seven greenhouses, a network of permanent raised beds, a diverse apple orchard, a sprawling herb garden, multiple specialty gardens, unique ecosystems, happy pigs, laying hens, and bees, bees, bees.

At the Inn at Bay Fortune we nurture, tend, and harvest two hundred or so varieties of vegetables, herbs, and specialty produce. We grow what we serve, but we harvest far more than impeccable produce from our soil. Our culinary farm has also grown into a living, breathing classroom. We learn by doing, by immersing ourselves, by simply connecting human beings to the soil their food comes from.

There are many types of farms in today's global food system, each with an integrity of its own. On Prince Edward Island alone we have large-scale commercial monoculture farms, smaller market garden farms, single-family subsistence farms, vineyards, orchards, dairy farms, livestock farms, and fish farms. On land, though, no matter the type, every farm begins with its soil.

As farmers we understand that our first responsibility is to our earth's ecosystem and its three basic cycles: water, nitrogen, and carbon. We naturally focus on the life of our plants, but they come and go while the life of the soil endures. Our systems continuously strengthen the incredibly diverse and productive microorganisms within that soil. Organic is just our starting line. With one foot planted in the past and another firmly in the future, we deploy a wide array of fascinating natural techniques to ensure the soil's long-term vitality. We're inspired by the circle of life: the ongoing connection between healthy soil, a healthy environment, and healthy, happy humans. We know that the more nutritious an ingredient is, the better it tastes and the better the earth it came from.

As cooks firmly rooted in the soil, we prize flavour and strive for diversity, nurturing two hundred or so different plant types annually. We're blessed with extravagant bounty, just-harvested freshness, a strengthening terroir of our own, and a daily connection to the rhythms and rituals of our farm that endures in our lifelong respect of vegetables we show through the art and craft of our cooking.

farmer kevin

Farmer Kevin Petrie personifies the ideals of our culinary farm. His personal passion, enduring enthusiasm, and growing patience help him lead the daily and annual rhythms of our farm. He's a well-informed communicator who can inspire a crowd with a blue-sky story or dive deep into a one-on-one conversation on the minutiae of a particular farming detail. He's devoted to his family, has a great dog, and struggles with his hockey team just like any normal guy. He's real.

One of modern agriculture's greatest challenges is the loss of that personal connection between the farmer and the consumer. So much is gained in our global food system—we're feeding our planet, after all—but much is lost too, and our farmers feel it more than we do. Absentee consumers can only ask the planet to do so much, and we often forget the people on the ground who our choices affect. We're all part of the same system, and farmers are just doing their best to meet demand.

Farmer Kevin reminds us that farming is always personal, and that our food choices matter somewhere other than our table. But perhaps his greatest strength is to show us that real action doesn't have to be scary, that each of us can choose an ethical path forward. At the inn we're blessed to farm the way we do, and we try not to judge the rest of the system we too are a part of. We simply choose to learn through action, to get moving, and to grow along the way. We're not anti anything, we're just pro-flavour!

We founded our culinary farm to grow the highest possible quality of fruits and vegetables of the widest possible variety. Not surprisingly we've discovered the very best flavour is found through the very best farming. The sustainable, regenerative agricultural practices that define Farmer Kevin's brand-new old-fashioned style have strengthened our soil and helped us create our own unique terroir. Those same strategies give our vegetables incredible flavour.

Every farm has a farmer. Look around and do your best to find some near you and learn their stories. Our innate human ability to connect with others helps us grow both as people and as cooks. Support your new friends—and tell them Farmer Kevin says hi!

sustainable, regenerative agriculture

The very essence of farming is to take from the soil, and sustainable, regenerative agriculture allows us to return more to the earth than we remove. This fundamental mindset guides our culinary farm and helps us grow the most flavourful vegetables we can. The results are obvious, but as with most things on the farm you have to dig a bit deeper to really understand the harvest.

Enlightened cooks pursue flavour for more than just the hedonistic delight of their guests. We're drawn to flavourful fruits and vegetables because they're healthy. We've long understood that we are what we eat, that we're at our best when we eat well. In fresh fruits and vegetables, the very molecules that add intense colour and flavour are also beneficial micronutrients. As their flavours peak, so does their nutritional intensity. The better they taste, the better they are for us. But that's not all great flavour means.

Through the rituals and rhythms of farming, we also understand the link between the flavours we seek, the underlying health of our soil, and the strength of its all-important mycorrhizal fungi. As we've built the strength of our own unique terroir, we've also built the strength of the flavours produced. Through our own hard work, we've learned one of life's most profound lessons: we belong to our planet more than it belongs to us.

"I grow soil, not vegetables," said Prince Edward Island's organic farming pioneer Paul Offer. I was a young chef holding his legendary rich soil in my hands, knowing I needed the best ingredients, but not yet knowing what that meant. Paul explained, but it took me years to really understand. The pursuit of flavour can be noble, but it can't be selfish. To truly enjoy today's flavours, we must graciously consider tomorrow too.

new old-fashioned farming

Farming is challenging. To succeed takes real patience, unwavering persistence, a colossal appetite for long, hard work, a long list of tried-and-true methods, and an appetite for new ones. The recipe also includes an intuitive understanding of "why we do it" well beyond "what we do." Not surprisingly, that knowledge is firmly rooted in the past.

For most of recorded history, agriculture was naturally sustainable because it had to be: it was local, and there was no other way. In the last one hundred years, though, we've perfected a global system by isolating the necessary fertilizing components—nitrogen, phosphorus, and potassium—then maximizing agricultural yield through large-scale industrial processes that we now know to be unsustainable. We fed a lot of people, but we also did a lot of damage to the planet.

Enlightened farmers think of their soil as a permanent partner and respect it in their own ways. On our farm we give it rich, nutritious mulch-based organic seafood compost, carefully mound it into neat, raised beds, and never turn it over again. This low-till system incorporates drainage channels in between the beds to prevent the adjacent roots from resting in waterlogged soil, while year after year the beneficial microbiology of the undisturbed beds only grows stronger. We even plant beneficial oats in the pathways between the beds to absorb water and suppress weeds. All of these practices were a common part of farming long before modern farming. Ancient wisdom that's just as applicable today as it ever was.

Some of our farm is devoted to perennial plantings, to plants that grow and flourish in one place year after year, happily symbiotic with their soil for all time. But most of the farm changes each year, and that progression can easily exhaust the soil. Through careful succession planting and crop rotation, we ensure that if a crop one year depletes a particular nutrient from the soil, we plant something the next year that gives it back.

In the winter we occultate—we deny light to the earth. We cover acres of our farm with thick black tarps instead of back-breaking seaweed. In the spring the soil warms quickly, and any lingering harmful seeds near the surface sprout, only to wither in the dark while the soil lives on. When we peel back the tarp to plant, we already have a huge head start on curtailing weeds. After years of effort, we've dramatically reduced the number of weeds that mingle with our crops. Success with yet another modern version of an old idea.

our prince edward island terroir

Terroir: both the unique ecosystem and the characteristic flavours of a specific growing area.

When you patiently grow your own vegetables, you learn to expect fresh, ripe flavour. The flavour of an ingredient grown mere feet from your table and harvested mere minutes ago is of course amazing, but there can be so much more.

Prince Edward Island is a giant green farm floating in the deep blue sea. Our iron-rich soil is legendary for the high-quality fruits and vegetables it produces. Our orchards, and vegetable and grain farms flourish, and even the cows that graze our pastures produce some of the highest milk fat percentages on the planet. Our farmers understand our connection to the earth around us.

Sustainable, regenerative agricultural practices help us respect our soil as a living, breathing partner. We've worked hard to strengthen our culinary farm's many and varied microbiological systems. Today our soil requires no chemical encouragement, it absorbs just the right amount of water, worms love it, and it's clearly found balance with our island environment. Every shovelful reveals a wildly varied and uniquely healthy ecosystem.

A few years ago, we gradually began to realize that our farm's flavours weren't just about the obvious impeccable freshness. There was a more intangible quality as well. Somehow the flavours of our vegetables have intensified and brightened, or maybe "deepened" is a better word. They taste more of themselves. They've grown, and so have we. We have created our own terroir. We have become stewards of our land.

In human terms, terroir connects us to time and place. In the past we were tethered to our environment of necessity, but today many of us have lost that meaningful connection. Through our food choices we can respect the long journey of farming while enjoying the fleeting flavours of the harvest. We ground our lives through the kitchen.

today's farm project

The Inn at Bay Fortune is blessed with a daily harvest of mind-boggling variety and quality. Our cooks watch a parade of fruits and vegetables come through the back door all season long. Every day they show their respect for the farm through their cooking. But that respect is not learned in the kitchen. True insight comes only when you get your hands dirty.

Every day at the inn starts on the farm. Every morning our chefs' brigade rallies with Farmer Kevin's team for the day's farm project. Every day's task is different, but we always work as a team and take on one big job. Eight of us can get far more done in one hour than one of us in eight hours, and anyway, it's way more fun together. We get energized, then we get cooking. Company's coming.

Our culinary farm may grow vegetables for our evening's guests, but all day long it educates and inspires our cooks. They've joined our brigade for that connection. Over the course of the season, the daily ritual of the farm project leads to many moments of profound personal growth and real pride in our harvest. "I grew that!" is the ultimate compliment from a cook as they describe flavours to a guest.

Our work always begins with a lesson from Farmer Kevin as he leads us through the details of the project. He helps us understand the "why"' behind the "what" and keeps our conversations lively. We learn the nuances of our farm—but we're still not sure about his hockey team.

We plant minuscule seeds, transplant tiny seedlings, build raised beds, build wheelbarrow brigades for composting, haul seaweed, straw bales, and organic mulch, lots of mulch. We plant long rows of variously spaced and precisely located vegetables, we weed like a SWAT team, roll tarps, hoe, rake, shovel, mow, and otherwise tend beds, and then after months of hard work we finally reap what we sow, we harvest with laser precision everything from tiny flower petals to giant winter squashes. And we learn about ourselves every single step of the way.

A year of sustainable, regenerative farming is a year of days, each unique and fleeting. A long annual rhythm of many micro moments intricately connected yet thrillingly individual. An evolving tapestry of flavours coming and going as each ingredient ripens. The daily work is real, and so is the reward when we're fully immersed in the moment.

life-cycle harvesting

A forgotten radish patch a few years back. A radish crop seemingly past its prime. A second season of snappy flower foraging. A random discovery of a tender seed pod. We're far from the first to discover the full potential of this plant, but when we did, it inspired a revolutionary new way of looking at our farm that endures: life-cycle harvesting.

In five days, a radish seed sprouts into a mildly snappy cotyledon, the plant's very first green growth. This microgreen is one of our favourite garnishes. In twenty days, we pluck a marble-sized radish with its long tail intact below and first tender greens attached above. At thirty days, we harvest a classic radish and its full greens. We have until day forty-five or so before the root toughens. After sixty days, the plant shifts from its vegetative state to a reproductive state and begins inexhaustibly producing spicy flowers. At ninety days, we pick tender green seed pods that rank among the most delicious vegetables we grow. By 120 days, the pods have matured and toughened and we can harvest the seeds. With sequential planting, the full life cycle of radishes becomes a part of our menu all season long.

We nurture hundreds of different types of plants from seed every year and often grow them until they yield seed yet again. Each plant progresses through its own micro-seasons as it germinates, sprouts, and shoots its way through its vegetative state to an eventual reproductive state. Along the way each fruit and vegetable reaches a point of ripe perfection, its flavours, colours, and textures ready for peak harvest. Some are with us for the season, some we harvest for weeks, others last mere days. Afterwards most become bitter and tough, yet many will eventually produce fragrant flowers and seeds, another daily reward for a full season's vigilance.

seeds,
the seed house,
and the
sprout house

Seeds are one of life's greatest miracles—a tiny, tough package of energy and information poised for explosive growth under just the right conditions. Fewer than half of our plants are perennial and permanent. The majority of our annual harvest begins as miniature seeds in our care. It's an immense task.

We maintain an extensive seed library of many hundreds of varietals. We meticulously keep track of what we plant and what we harvest. Our seeds come from a variety of trusted sources (see page 229). We prize diversity and we're forever trying new types. We've even dedicated our trial garden to finding the best seeds for our terroir.

We bring many of our seeds to life in late winter in our seed house. We precisely insert them in sprouting medium, then rest them in a thick layer of gently warmed sand atop a timber-framed bench. Within days they sprout, beginning their journey to harvest. Naturally they expand exponentially, so by early spring our row-cover tunnel greenhouses are packed with plants ready for post-frost planting.

As the season progresses, we also sow seeds directly in the earth. Meanwhile, many of our edible flower beds seed themselves and thus return year after year in the same place. To encourage their future growth, we give them lots of room and harvest them selectively. Other delicious seeds emerge towards the end of a plant's life cycle. Fresh licorice-flavoured fennel seeds and tender green coriander seeds are among our very best flavours.

In our sprout house we explore yet another use for seeds. Here, seeds sprout into tiny edible cotyledons that are delicious in their own right. Our soil-free stainless-steel system is unlike any other on the farm, but it's a daily source of snappy, bright flavour.

the herb house and herb garden

Herbs contribute so much in the kitchen that naturally we try to grow them all, every varietal of every type, more than one hundred at last count.

Our herb garden cascades down our front lawn in a series of raised timber-framed beds, each six foot square. Each bed is dedicated to a single herb, and most are perennials that strengthen every year. We established this edible treasure trove mere steps from the kitchen to inspire the creativity of our chefs. And inspired they were: already we have forty-six beds.

As you wander the whimsical grounds of the inn, you'll spot strategic plantings of even more herbs, many tucked away for our farm bar's use. Sage bushes here, eight types of mint there, even a thirty-year-old seven-foot-high lovage plant. On our upper farm we've built a further system of long beds for the herbs we use most: chives, sorrel, anise hyssop, lavender, thyme, cicely, oregano, and lovage. Basil gets the rock-star treatment, with hundreds of dedicated bed feet.

None of these plants, however, are ready when we open in May each year. And so our herb house is dedicated to an indoor collection of essential herbs that come alive very quickly in the spring, fast enough to get us up and running long before the outdoor beds fully warm up: sage, thyme, various mints, lemon balm, chives, savory, tarragon, oregano, and an ongoing fennel plant experiment. On sunny winter days it's very warm inside; the soil lays dormant but never freezes. We go even further for perennial rosemary and lemon verbena, two of our favourites that need delicate Mediterranean treatment. In the winter they're insulated inside smaller, precisely warmed greenhouses built around their individual beds.

the mushroom patch project

One of the foundations of our culinary farm is our own growth as farmers and stewards of our land. As our roots have deepened, we've challenged ourselves to continue broadening our diversity with new projects every year. Now we're digital everything, deploying high-efficiency irrigation systems, expanding our energy-friendly greenhouses, and actively exploring alternative wind and solar power. We've welcomed happy pigs, our own flock of laying hens, and rows of super-helpful beehives. Our woodlands are bearing fruit too, and we're brewing old-fashioned hard cider from our own wild apple trees. Meanwhile, in the shade, we're really going deep.

In the winter, once the wood is infused with a full season's nutrients, we harvest local maple logs. In the spring we bore precise holes in the logs and insert sawdust plugs inoculated with living mushroom spores. We brush the holes with paraffin wax to tightly seal in the beneficial ecosystem, arrange the logs in the shade at the edge of the farm, mere steps into the forest, then hope for the best. Over the next year or so, the mycelium—a web of fine filaments that serves to nourish the mushrooms—colonizes the log and eventually begins poking its fruiting bodies up through the holes, and our very own mushrooms emerge. With selective harvesting, each log bears fruit for many years. That continuing harvest makes growing mushrooms an incredibly efficient part of our culinary farm.

Sometimes you must leap into the unknown and hope for the best. It can take a year or more for a mushroom log to bear fruit and to establish an annual cycle, so we had to add more logs before the first ones bore fruit. That's plenty of time to consider the real lessons learned, patience and persistence.

When we founded our culinary farm, none of us could imagine how far we'd grow, but we could imagine trying to get a little better every day, season by season. We planted the seeds for real growth by encouraging our own constant evolution and harvesting knowledge as much as vegetables.

The
MUSHROOM
PATCH

happy animals

Farm animals and livestock have long played a significant role in traditional agriculture and can be an integral part of modern sustainable farming too. Climate change concerns us all, and our collective food choices have a huge effect on the environment. Large-scale meat production is particularly challenging, so a plant-based food system is quickly growing. There will be a continuing place for meat, but there will be less of it. Animals have always deserved our respect, and as our tastes continue to evolve, they can still thrive within a diverse and balanced ecosystem.

Every year three pigs join our farm team for the season. They have one job, and they're good at it: to live a happy life. They're fed mostly organic grain and vegetable scraps from the kitchen. They love nothing better than rooting in the earth, breaking the sod for us so we can build yet another permanent raised bed. Our cooks watch them grow until one day they're gone. But they're not forgotten. We honour the connection made and respect earned through better food choices and a freezer full of lovingly smoked ham for next year.

We maintain a flock of laying hens so our breakfast guests can enjoy farm-fresh flavour. Our chickens have their own tractor, a pen-on-wheels that moves twice a day to a fresh patch of grassy goodness where they happily peck away at the sweet salad, bugs, and grubs in the soil while granting us eggs each day. Not surprisingly, these outside hens lay eggs with far more flavour than those of their inside friends.

Bees happily volunteer for one of the single most essential tasks on our farm: merrily pollinating vast swathes of our fruits and vegetables for us. We're useless without them and lucky they love our farm. We site a row of tall hives in a safe place and plant pollinators—marigolds, borage, nasturtiums, and flowering herbs—throughout the farm to attract bees to every corner. Amazingly they pay us for the privilege, and we're rewarded with an annual bounty of rich, fragrant honey.

trial garden

We all need to plan for our future, to try new things without being afraid to fail. Our culinary farm may be near the far eastern tip of Canada's smallest province, nestled along the shore of Prince Edward Island, but we are not isolated. The world around us is moving quickly, our climate is changing, and people's tastes are evolving. Our trial garden gives us a safe place to experiment.

Most of our fruits and vegetables are perfectly at home in our zone 5B North American climate because sustainable, regenerative farming always works in harmony with its local climate. We extend our growing season by building greenhouses and nurturing plants indoors, ready for the soil the moment the risk of frost has passed. We don't farm like we're in the tropics, but we can try.

The incredible flavour of a warm, juicy, fragrant just-picked sun-ripened heirloom tomato inspires many northern farmers to grow this southern fruit. The plant thrives in long, hot summers, but some varieties tolerate the Island's shorter sunny season. There are hundreds of seed types to choose from, so we patiently trial new varieties to see which give us the best flavour from our terroir. Some never ripen, so we've learned to celebrate the taste of failure as we preserve a variety of inevitable green tomato condiments at season's end.

Much of our farm effort is dedicated to our glorious Farmer's Salad. We often share a festive bowl filled with more than fifty distinct ingredients. Our greens base always includes lots of tender greens, leaves, and lettuces. The world loves salad, so we're blessed with a steady stream of innovative new seeds to try every year. With our data-tracking system, we log every step of a new plant's growth to guide our future planting.

When we began our culinary farm, the entire project was a trial garden. We've grown and evolved, we've stumbled onto systems, invented techniques, perfected methods, created our own terroir, and learned the biggest lesson of all: never stop learning. We've built a strong base but not a plateau, so we keep climbing. Our most important harvest is knowledge, so we continue to refine what we've already learned while remaining open to the new lessons ahead.

farmhouse
vegetarian

sorrel hummus

sourdough crackers, sumac chili oil

Every cook has a favourite dip for the sunny sweetness of farm-fresh vegetables. Hummus is ours. We make this simple, healthy snack with a variety of fresh green garden herbs like basil, mint, cilantro, tarragon, or parsley. This recipe uses sorrel, which adds a bright boost of distinctly sour citric-like flavour. The plant's younger tender leaves often appear in our daily salad blend, while the older leaves are puréed raw or lightly wilted. Sumac is a classic hummus garnish. We forage staghorn sumac berries in the early summer. After drying, they're ground into a fragrant purple powder with a citric-sour flavour all its own.

Our breads are naturally fermented, so our bakery always has lots of extra sourdough starter for a batch of fresh crackers. If you don't have any extra starter, though, simply combine flour with water, or dive in with your favourite crackers.

Make the Sumac Chili Oil
In a small saucepan, combine the vegetable oil and chili flakes and heat over medium heat until the temperature reaches 350°F (180°C). Remove from the heat and let sit until cool, 4 hours or so. Whisk in the sumac. Transfer to a mason jar or resealable container. Cover tightly and rest at room temperature overnight before using. Store, covered, at room temperature for up to 1 month.

Make the Sourdough Crackers
Arrange the racks in the upper and lower thirds of the oven and preheat to 350°F (180°C). Turn on the convection fan if you have one. Line 2 baking sheets with parchment paper or a silicone baking mat.

In a medium bowl, stir together the sourdough starter, whole wheat flour, and olive oil. Knead into a ball of smooth dough. Divide into 2 portions. On a lightly floured work surface, use a rolling pin to roll out each portion as thinly as possible. Transfer the dough to the baking sheets. Evenly sprinkle with kosher salt. Bake until golden brown and crispy, 20 minutes or so. Cool the crackers on the baking sheets, then break into large pieces before serving. Store in a resealable container at room temperature for up to 3 days.

Make the Sorrel Hummus
In a food processor, combine the sorrel, garlic, chickpeas, lemon zest and juice, tahini, olive oil, water, sea salt, and chili powder. Blend until smooth. Transfer the hummus to a resealable container and store in the refrigerator for up to 3 days. Serve in a festive bowl or spoon onto a decorative platter. Drizzle with sumac chili oil. Serve with an array of fresh vegetables and sourdough crackers.

Sumac Chili Oil

1 cup (250 mL) vegetable oil

¼ cup (60 mL) Red Chili Flakes (page 219) or store-bought

¼ cup (60 mL) ground sumac

Sourdough Crackers

1 cup (250 mL) sourdough starter (or mix together 1 cup/ 250 mL whole wheat flour and 1 cup/250 mL water; use 1 cup/250 mL of this mixture)

1 cup (250 mL) whole wheat flour

¼ cup (60 mL) olive oil

2 teaspoons (10 mL) kosher salt (we use Windsor)

Sorrel Hummus (makes 2 cups/500 mL)

2 cups (500 mL) fresh sorrel leaves (2 ounces/57 g)

2 large garlic cloves, minced

1 can (19 ounces/540 g) chickpeas, drained and rinsed

Zest and juice of 1 lemon

½ cup (125 mL) tahini

¼ cup (60 mL) extra-virgin olive oil

¼ cup (60 mL) water

½ teaspoon (2 mL) sea salt

Pinch of chili powder

1 pound (450 g) of your favourite fresh baby vegetables for dipping (such as green beans, yellow beans, edible-pod peas, carrots, turnips, radishes, cucumbers)

vegetable broth and vegetable tea

Makes about 3 quarts (3 L)

In today's kitchen a go-to vegetable broth is an essential pantry staple. Vegetables release their flavourful essence much quicker than tougher meats and proteins. Quick cooking elevates their flavours, but long cooking can mute them. Root vegetables are the exception, but anything green will eventually fade, and with their colour goes flavour and nutrition. Minimal simmering and patient steeping off the heat, plus a finishing flavour boost, all help build a delicious vegetable broth.

If you're riffing with what you have on hand, keep in mind that some ingredients don't belong in vegetable broth. Use your kitchen's best scraps, peels, and leftovers. Avoid the bitter brassica family: broccoli, cauliflower, cabbage, and Brussels sprouts. Green vegetables lose their colour and make the liquid murky. Beets add too much of their colour. Potatoes, sweet potatoes, and squashes dissolve quickly and cloud the broth.

For an enjoyable restorative tea, you can further flavour the broth by steeping fresh herbs in it, adding aromatic complexity and therapeutic benefits.

Make the Vegetable Broth

Pour the water and wine into a large pot. Add the bay leaves, fennel seeds, coriander seeds, peppercorns, and salt. Bring to a full furious boil over high heat, then reduce the heat to a slow, steady simmer. Add the mushrooms, carrots, celery, parsnips, fennel, onions, and garlic. Stir gently once. Cover and simmer over low heat for 30 minutes.

Remove from the heat. Add the parsley, thyme, and reserved fennel fronds, gently pushing them below the surface. Cover and rest for 1 hour. Strain the broth through a fine-mesh strainer or standard strainer lined with several layers of folded cheesecloth into a large bowl. To ensure a clear broth, avoid pressing on the vegetables but shake gently instead. Discard the solids. Reserve the broth, or transfer to a resealable container and refrigerate for up to 1 week or freeze for up to 6 months.

Make the Vegetable Tea

Fill a 4-cup (1 L) mason jar or several smaller clear glasses with handfuls of fresh herb sprigs, flowers, or leaves. Pour enough vegetable broth to fill the jar or glasses into a small pot and bring to a full simmer. Pour the hot broth over the herbs. Enjoy immediately, sipping slowly and savouring the aromatic nuances, or transfer to a resealable container and refrigerate for up to 1 week.

Vegetable Broth

3 quarts (3 L) water

2 cups (500 mL) dry white wine

4 bay leaves

1 tablespoon (15 mL) fennel seeds

1 tablespoon (15 mL) coriander seeds

1 tablespoon (15 mL) black peppercorns

1 tablespoon (15 mL) sea salt

1 pound (450 g) white mushrooms, sliced

4 carrots, peeled and coarsely grated

4 celery stalks, thinly sliced

2 large parsnips, peeled and coarsely grated

1 fennel bulb, trimmed, halved, cored, and thinly sliced, feathery fronds reserved

2 large white onions, thinly sliced

Cloves from 1 head of garlic

A handful of fresh parsley sprigs

6 sprigs of fresh thyme

Vegetable Tea

Hot Vegetable Broth (recipe above)

A few handfuls of your favourite fresh herb sprigs, flowers, or leaves (use a single favourite or try a variety of complementary ones: sage, rosemary, and thyme; tarragon and thyme; lemon verbena and lemon balm; lavender and mint)

shiitake gai lan noodle bowl

umami broth, enoki nori tarragon tangle

This bowl, as much salad as soup, is packed with hearty, satisfying flavour but not heaviness. You'll enjoy brightly flavoured fresh vegetables and slurpy, chewy noodles in a full-bodied vegetable broth. Umami is the savouriness so characteristic of meat that we so often crave. It can also be coaxed from shiitake mushrooms, fermented soy, and nori seaweed sheets. In this recipe, their collective richness is balanced by sharp tarragon and sweet, pleasingly bitter gai lan (Chinese-style broccoli). This savoury green vegetable can be enjoyed simply steamed or lightly grilled and charred for even more savouriness.

Cook the Noodles

Bring a large pot of unsalted water to a full boil. Cook the noodles until nearly tender, 4 to 5 minutes. Drain in a colander and rinse well under cold running water, stirring gently with your hand, until cool. Divide the noodles evenly among bowls.

Grill the Gai Lan

Build and tend an aromatic fire in your firepit, burning down to a thick bed of glowing hot coals. Alternatively, fire up your barbecue or grill.

Carefully place the gai lan on grates and grill, turning and repositioning occasionally, until bright green, tender, and lightly charred, 5 minutes or so. Remove to a cutting board and cut 3 or 4 times crosswise into bite-size pieces. Divide evenly among the bowls with noodles.

Toss the Enoki Nori Tarragon Tangle

In a large bowl, gently toss together the enoki mushrooms, nori, green onions, tarragon, and sesame seeds.

Make the Umami Broth

Heat the vegetable oil in a large saucepan over medium-high heat. Add the shiitake mushrooms, onion, and garlic and cook, stirring frequently, just long enough to fully heat through the vegetables and brighten their flavours, 2 or 3 minutes. Season with salt. Add the vegetable broth, sake, soy sauce, and rice vinegar and bring to a quick simmer. Ladle the broth evenly over the noodles and grilled gai lan. Sprinkle with sesame oil. Top with a handful of enoki nori tarragon tangle. Enjoy with chopsticks.

Serves 4 as a vegetarian meal or 8 as a side

Shiitake Gai Lan Noodle Bowl

1 package (14 ounces/400 g) dry soba noodles

1 bunch of gai lan, yu choy, or bok choy (about 1 pound/ 450 g)

2 tablespoons (30 mL) vegetable oil

8 ounces (225 g) shiitake mushrooms, stems removed, thinly sliced

1 white onion, thinly sliced

2 garlic cloves, thinly sliced

Sea salt

4 cups (1 L) Vegetable Broth (page 34) or water

1 cup (250 mL) sake

2 teaspoons (10 mL) dark soy sauce

1 teaspoon (5 mL) rice vinegar

Toasted sesame oil, for sprinkling

Enoki Nori Tarragon Tangle

1 bunch of enoki mushrooms (3 to 4 ounces/85 to 115 g), torn into individual strands

1 large nori sheet, cut into 4 long strips, stacked, and finely slivered crosswise using scissors

2 green onions, cut diagonally into thin slivers

Leaves from 4 sprigs of fresh tarragon

¼ cup (60 mL) sesame seeds

radish, smashed cucumber, tofu, and hemp heart salad

borage flowers, salad burnet, garden tangle, preserved lemon dressing

Sharp radish, cool cucumber, smooth tofu, and richly nutritious hemp hearts balance this salad with an interplay of textures and tastes. Together they're a thematic flavour base for a riotous tangle of bright, complementary herbs and tender sprouts. Borage flowers and salad burnet leaves both have cucumber-like aromatic flavours. Tender radish sprouts add a burst of pleasant sharpness. All are tied together with a bright lemony dressing. A summer garden's best in a bowl!

Make the Smashed Cucumbers

Cut the cucumbers in half lengthwise. Lay each half cut side down on the cutting board. Lay the blade of a large knife flat across the cucumber and with your other hand press down firmly until the skin cracks and the cucumber fractures. Work your way down the full length. Cut or break into bite-size pieces and transfer to a small bowl. Toss the cucumbers with the salt and sugar, then transfer to a small strainer and position over the bowl to drain thoroughly, 30 minutes or so.

Prepare the Garden Tangle

Lightly toss together the borage, burnet, and radish sprouts.

Finish the Salad

Transfer the drained cucumbers to a large bowl. Add the radishes, tofu, hemp hearts, and preserved lemon dressing. Lightly toss until thoroughly combined. Top with the garden tangle.

Serves 4 as a vegetarian meal or 8 as a side

Radish, Smashed Cucumber, Tofu, and Hemp Heart Salad

2 English cucumbers

1 teaspoon (5 mL) kosher salt (we use Windsor)

1 teaspoon (5 mL) sugar

6 ounces (170 g) radishes, trimmed and quartered

1 daikon radish, peeled and coarsely grated

1 block (12 ounces/340 g) firm tofu, drained and cut into 1-inch (2.5 cm) cubes

1 cup (250 mL) hemp hearts

½ cup (125 mL) Preserved Lemon Dressing (page 220)

Garden Tangle

50 or so fresh borage flowers

A handful or two of fresh salad burnet leaves

A handful or two of fresh radish sprouts

tomatoes, nasturtiums, and golden halloumi

honey dressing

When tomatoes are at their peak on our farm, they're surrounded by flavourful salad mates. Various basils, fresh herbs, and marigolds are all worthy of co-starring with impeccable sun-ripe tomatoes in a deeply flavourful salad. In this bowl, peppery nasturtium leaves and flowers balance the medley of flavours in our season's best tomatoes. We love their bright colours, but their distinctive sharp flavour is what makes this combo memorable. The aromatic complexity of the honey dressing adds complementary floral notes.

Make the Honey Dressing
Measure the canola oil, lemon zest and juice, honey, mustard, and salt into a 2-cup (500 mL) mason jar. Screw on the lid and shake vigorously into a smooth dressing. Alternatively, whisk everything together in a small bowl. Reserve or cover tightly and refrigerate for up to 1 week. Shake or whisk again before using.

Pan-Fry the Halloumi
Cut the halloumi into thick slices. Stack the slices, a few at a time, and cut into large bite-size cubes. Heat the vegetable oil in a large non-stick skillet over medium-high heat. Fry the cheese cubes, turning occasionally and adjusting the heat to maintain a steady sizzle, until evenly browned all over, 10 minutes or so. Transfer the halloumi to a plate lined with paper towel to absorb excess oil.

Assemble the Salad
Gather the tomatoes and nasturtium leaves in a large festive bowl. Add the golden halloumi and the honey dressing. Lightly toss until fully combined. Top with nasturtium flowers.

Serves 4 as a vegetarian meal or 8 as a side

Honey Dressing

½ cup (125 mL) extra-virgin canola or olive oil

Zest and juice of 2 lemons

¼ cup (60 mL) of your favourite local artisanal honey (see page 229)

1 tablespoon (15 mL) Dijon mustard

½ teaspoon (2 mL) sea salt

Tomatoes, Nasturtiums, and Golden Halloumi

18 ounces (500 g) halloumi cheese

2 tablespoons (30 mL) vegetable oil

2 pounds (900 g) sun-ripe heirloom tomatoes, several varietals, halved, quartered, or sliced into bite-size pieces

50 fresh nasturtium leaves (about 2 ounces/57 g)

25 fresh nasturtium flowers (about 2 ounces/57 g)

shiitake cabbage tacos

green lentil smear, green jam

These richly flavoured tacos balance the earthiness of shiitake mushrooms and green lentils with the sweetness of cabbage, the sourness of green tomatoes, and the distinctive flavour of an aromatic treat from our herb garden. Green coriander seeds are the tender immature seeds of the cilantro plant. Before they dry, their flavours are intensely sweet and fresh. Their brief season is preserved in this distinctive jam. Green tomatoes are a regular part of our farm too—not every tomato ripens in our Canadian climate!

Makes 16 or so large tacos

Green Jam

1 cup (250 mL) apple cider vinegar

½ cup (125 mL) sugar

1 teaspoon (5 mL) sea salt

1 teaspoon (5 mL) Red Chili Flakes (page 219) or store-bought

1 pound (450 g) green tomatoes, quartered

1 large white onion, thinly sliced

1 jalapeño pepper, stem and seeds removed, minced

¼ cup (60 mL) green coriander seeds (or 2 tablespoons/30 mL dried coriander seeds)

Green Lentil Smear

2 tablespoons (30 mL) butter or vegetable oil

1 tablespoon (15 mL) cumin seeds

1 large yellow onion, minced

4 garlic cloves, minced

1 cup (250 mL) green lentils

3 cups (750 mL) water

1 bay leaf

1 teaspoon (5 mL) sea salt

Shiitake Cabbage Tacos

1 savoy, white, or green cabbage

Sea salt

Freshly ground pepper

2 tablespoons (30 mL) vegetable oil

2 tablespoons (30 mL) butter or more vegetable oil

1 pound (450 g) shiitake mushrooms, stems removed, larger caps halved

1 teaspoon (5 mL) soy sauce

1 teaspoon (5 mL) pure liquid honey

1 bunch (3 to 4 ounces/85 to 115 g) enoki mushrooms

A handful of fresh cilantro sprigs

Make the Green Jam

Measure the apple cider vinegar, sugar, salt, and chili flakes into a medium saucepan. (If using dried coriander seeds, add them now.) Bring the pickling liquid to a full boil over medium-high heat. Add the green tomatoes, onion, and jalapeño. Bring to a slow, steady simmer and continue cooking, stirring frequently, until the mixture thickens and reduces, 15 minutes or so. Remove from the heat. Stir in the green coriander seeds, reserving a few for garnish. Serve warm or at room temperature, or store in a resealable container in the refrigerator for up to 1 week.

recipe continues

Make the Green Lentil Smear

Toss the butter into a medium saucepan over medium-high heat. Swirl gently as it melts, foams, and eventually lightly browns. Reduce the heat to low and stir in the cumin seeds. Continue stirring as their flavours emerge and brighten and the seeds lightly toast, about 1 minute. Stir in the onion and garlic. Cover tightly and cook, stirring occasionally, until the vegetables are soft and fragrant, 2 or 3 minutes more. Stir in the lentils, water, bay leaf, and salt. Bring to a slow, steady simmer, cover tightly, and cook for 20 minutes. Without uncovering, remove from the heat and let sit for another 10 minutes. In a food processor, purée the lentil mixture until smooth. Serve warm or at room temperature. Store in a covered container in the refrigerator for up to 3 days.

Prepare the Cabbage Leaves

Cut the cabbage through the stem, first in half, then into quarters. Evenly season the cut faces of the cabbage with salt and pepper.

Heat a large cast-iron skillet, plancha, griddle, or non-stick skillet over medium-high heat to precisely 350°F (180°C). For best results use a surface thermometer. Add the vegetable oil to the pan. Position the cabbage wedges in the pan so a cut side is in full contact with the cooking surface. If you're using a skillet, tightly cover it. Cook, turning occasionally as the cabbage gently sizzles and lightly caramelizes. Eventually the steamy moisture will work its way into the middle and tenderize it, 20 to 30 minutes. Remove the cabbage from the pan and rest until cool enough to handle. Trim away the tough core and separate the individual leaves.

Sauté the Mushrooms

Melt the butter in a large skillet over medium-high heat. Add the shiitake mushrooms and sauté just until tender but not browned, 5 minutes or so. Add the soy sauce and honey and continue cooking until combined, another minute or so. Remove from the heat. Serve warm or at room temperature.

Assemble the Tacos

Lay the cabbage leaves on a work surface. Spread a spoonful of the lentil smear on each leaf. Top with shiitake mushrooms and a dollop of green jam. Sprinkle with a few enoki mushrooms, tender cilantro sprigs, and reserved green coriander seeds.

beets, fire grains, and fresh ricotta with rosemary

Beets are among the sweetest vegetables we grow on the farm. Their deep, earthy flavour and natural sweetness make them versatile too— crisp and raw, roasted and caramelized, or brightly puréed. In this recipe, three beet types are balanced with rich, freshly made cheese, and hearty whole grains. Freekeh is made from green durum wheat that's fire-roasted to burn off chaff, then sun-dried and cracked, giving it a smoky toasted flavour to go with its memorable name.

Make the Fire Grains

In a small saucepan, combine the freekeh, water, salt, and bay leaves. Bring to a full boil over medium-high heat, then reduce the heat to a slow, steady simmer, cover tightly, and continue cooking until the water is absorbed and the grains are tender, 20 minutes or so. Without uncovering, remove from the heat and let sit for 10 minutes. Reserve or transfer to a resealable container and refrigerate for up to 3 days.

Roast the Beets

Preheat the oven to 425°F (220°C). Turn on the convection fan if you have one.

Set aside 1 of each beet type for use raw, 2 or 3 total. Reserve 1 pound (450 g) of red beets for the purée. The remaining red and yellow beets are for roasting. Reserve any beet greens for wilting.

Trim and reserve the stems from the roasting beets. Cut the beets into quarters and transfer to a 13 x 9-inch (3.5 L) baking dish. Toss the beets with the vegetable oil, ½ teaspoon (2 mL) of the salt, and pepper. Add ¼ cup (60 mL) of the water and cover tightly with foil. Bake until the beets are tender, 30 minutes or so. Remove the foil and continue baking, gently shaking the pan occasionally, until the water evaporates and the beets are lightly caramelized, 15 minutes or so more. Remove from the oven and rest the beets in the baking dish until cool enough to handle.

recipe continues

Serves 4 as a vegetarian meal or 8 as a side

Fire Grains

1 cup (250 mL) cracked freekeh

2½ cups (625 mL) water

¼ teaspoon (1 mL) sea salt

2 bay leaves

Raw, Roasted, and Puréed Beets

1 pound (450 g) red beets and their greens, washed, divided

2 pounds (900 g) yellow or heirloom beets (or more red beets) and their greens, washed, divided

2 tablespoons (30 mL) vegetable oil

1½ teaspoons (7 mL) sea salt, divided

Lots of freshly ground pepper

¾ cup (175 mL) water, divided

½ teaspoon (2 mL) ground cardamom

½ teaspoon (2 mL) of your favourite hot sauce

2 tablespoons (30 mL) extra-virgin canola or olive oil

1 tablespoon (15 mL) sherry vinegar or red wine vinegar

2 cups (500 mL) or so Fresh Ricotta with Rosemary (page 225)

Make the Beet Purée

Trim and reserve the stems from the reserved 1 pound (450 g) red beets. Wearing gloves to minimize staining, peel the beets. Using a juicer, juice half of the beets until you have ½ cup (125 mL) of juice. Strain the juice through a fine-mesh sieve into a cup or bowl. Discard the pulp. Quarter the remaining beets. Transfer the beets and beet juice, cardamom, hot sauce, and ½ teaspoon (2 mL) of the salt to a small saucepan over medium-high heat. Cover tightly, reduce the heat, and slowly simmer until tender, 15 minutes or so. Transfer to a high-speed blender. Add the canola oil and sherry vinegar. Purée until silky smooth. Taste and adjust seasoning. Reserve or transfer to a resealable container and refrigerate for up to 3 days.

Finish the Dish

Dice the reserved beet stems. Place the stems and the beet leaves in a saucepan with the remaining ½ cup (125 mL) water and the remaining ½ teaspoon (2 mL) salt. Bring to a steady simmer over medium heat, then cover tightly and cook until tender, 5 minutes or so. Remove from the heat. Use a slotted spoon to remove the beet stems and leaves from the saucepan as you serve.

Peel and thinly slice the reserved raw whole beets. Spoon the beet purée onto a serving platter or individual plates. Arrange the roasted beets, raw beet slices, and wilted beet greens with spoonfuls of the fire grains and fresh ricotta with rosemary.

lentil soup

pea and mint fritters, lentil sprouts

As hull-less red lentils simmer they break down into a rustic purée characteristic of the vast and colourful cuisine of India. This brightly flavoured version of dal is elevated further with crispy yet tender fritters. Chickpea flour is the secret ingredient that binds together garden-fresh green peas and cooling mint in an easily fried fritter batter. This spectacular soup is packed with more than enough flavour for a full meal!

Serves 4 as a vegetarian meal or 8 as a side

Lentil Soup

2 tablespoons (30 mL) coconut oil, vegetable oil, or butter

1 tablespoon (15 mL) curry powder

1 tablespoon (15 mL) sweet paprika

1 tablespoon (15 mL) coriander seeds

1 tablespoon (15 mL) cumin seeds

1 tablespoon (15 mL) fennel seeds

1 teaspoon (5 mL) Red Chili Flakes (page 219) or store-bought

2 white onions, diced

4 garlic cloves, minced

1½ cups (375 mL) red lentils

2 carrots, peeled and coarsely grated

4 cups (1 L) Vegetable Broth (page 34), store-bought, or water

1 can (14 ounces/398 mL) full-fat coconut milk

Zest and juice of 1 lemon

2 teaspoons (10 mL) sea salt

1 cup (250 mL) fresh Lentil Sprouts (see page 222), for garnish

Pea and Mint Fritters

3 cups (750 mL) fresh or frozen peas, divided

1 cup (250 mL) water

2 tablespoons (30 mL) butter or vegetable oil

2 cups (500 mL) chickpea flour

½ teaspoon (2 mL) sea salt

½ teaspoon (2 mL) baking soda

Leaves from 1 bunch of fresh mint, tightly rolled and thinly sliced

4 cups (1 L) vegetable oil, for frying

Make the Lentil Soup

Melt the coconut oil in a large pot over medium heat. Add the curry powder, paprika, coriander seeds, cumin seeds, fennel seeds, and chili flakes. Stir as their flavours brighten and intensify, just a minute or two. Add the onions and garlic and continue to stir and cook until the onions are soft and translucent, 5 minutes or so. Stir in the lentils, carrots, vegetable broth, and coconut milk. Bring to a full furious boil, then reduce the heat to a slow, steady simmer. Cover tightly and cook until the lentils are tender, 15 minutes or so.

Remove from the heat. Add the lemon zest and juice, salt and vigorously whisk the soup to break down the lentils. For an even smoother texture, purée the works in a high-speed blender or with an immersion blender. Return to the pot. Reheat just before serving.

Make the Pea and Mint Fritters

In a small saucepan, combine 1 cup (250 mL) of the peas, the water, and butter and bring to a slow, steady simmer over medium heat. Cook, stirring occasionally, until bright green and tender, just 2 minutes or so. Purée the works in a high-speed blender or with an immersion blender until smooth.

recipe continues

Whisk together the chickpea flour, salt, and baking soda in a medium bowl. Pour in the green pea purée, stirring until a smooth batter forms. Stir in the remaining 2 cups (500 mL) peas and the mint.

To fry the fritters, heat the vegetable oil in a large pot or deep-fryer over medium-high heat until it reaches 375°F (190°C) on a deep-fat thermometer. Using 2 spoons, the first to scoop, the second to release the batter, gently drop large dollops of the batter into the hot oil. Work in batches so you don't crowd the pot. Adjust the heat to maintain the ideal frying temperature of 365°F (185°C). Fry, stirring gently with a skimmer or slotted spoon, until the fritters are golden brown and tender, 3 to 5 minutes. Drain briefly on paper towel. Once the oil has returned to temperature, repeat with the remaining batter. (Cool, strain, and refrigerate the frying oil so you can use it again.)

Finish the Soup

Evenly ladle the soup into festive bowls. Top with a few fritters and a tangle of lentil sprouts.

kabocha squash and ancho cider broth

sage, pumpkin seed, and goat cheese pesto, spicy roasted chickpeas

Kabocha squash has a savoury yet deeply sweet flavour that ranks it among the tastiest vegetables on our farm. In this dish it braises till tender in a mulled cider broth rich with spices and aromatic ancho chilies, the dried version of fresh poblano pepper. We prize their medium heat that allows spice flavours to emerge without an overwhelming spicy heat. A classic pesto completes the presentation, melting into the broth with creamy goat cheese and fragrant sage.

Serves 4 as a vegetarian meal or 8 as a side

Spicy Roasted Chickpeas

1 can (19 ounces/540 g) chickpeas, drained and rinsed

2 tablespoons (30 mL) vegetable oil

1 tablespoon (15 mL) dark brown sugar

1 teaspoon (5 mL) smoked paprika

1 teaspoon (5 mL) chili powder

½ teaspoon (2 mL) Red Chili Flakes (page 219) or store-bought

½ teaspoon (2 mL) sea salt

Sage, Pumpkin Seed, and Goat Cheese Pesto

1 cup (250 mL) unsalted roasted pumpkin seeds

Leaves from 2 bunches of fresh sage (about 1 cup/250 mL)

4 garlic cloves, thinly sliced

¼ cup (60 mL) extra-virgin canola or olive oil

½ teaspoon (2 mL) sea salt

¼ teaspoon (1 mL) Red Chili Flakes (page 219) or store-bought

4 ounces (115 g) soft goat cheese

Kabocha Squash and Ancho Cider Broth

1 large kabocha squash or butternut squash (about 4 pounds/1.8 kg), unpeeled

1 tablespoon (15 mL) cumin seeds

1 tablespoon (15 mL) coriander seeds

4 cups (1 L) fresh apple cider or apple juice

1 cup (250 mL) Double Hill Nomad Cider (see page 229), your favourite hard cider, a crisp Riesling, or any other white or red wine

1 tablespoon (15 mL) apple cider vinegar

2 teaspoons (10 mL) sea salt

1 teaspoon (5 mL) cinnamon

¼ teaspoon (1 mL) ground allspice

Cloves from 1 head of garlic, peeled and halved

2 or 3 dried ancho chilies, stems and seeds removed, broken into small pieces

Make the Spicy Roasted Chickpeas

Preheat the oven to 400°F (200°C). Turn on the convection fan if you have one. Line a baking sheet with parchment paper or a silicone baking mat.

In a small bowl, stir together the chickpeas and vegetable oil. Spread in a single layer on the prepared baking sheet. Bake, stirring often, until lightly browned and crispy, 30 minutes or so.

recipe continues

Meanwhile, in a medium bowl, whisk together the brown sugar, paprika, chili powder, chili flakes, and salt. When the chickpeas are done, add them to the spice blend and toss until evenly coated. Reserve or transfer to a resealable container and store at room temperature for up to 1 week.

Make the Sage, Pumpkin Seed, and Goat Cheese Pesto
In a food processor, combine the pumpkin seeds, sage, garlic, canola oil, salt, and chili flakes. Process into a smooth purée, scraping down the sides once or twice. Add the goat cheese and process until smooth. Reserve or transfer to a resealable container and refrigerate for up to 3 days.

Make the Kabocha Squash and Ancho Cider Broth
Cut the squash in half lengthwise, remove the seeds and stem, and cut into large bite-size chunks. Combine the cumin seeds and coriander seeds in a large pot. Stir over medium heat until the seeds are fragrant, just a minute or so. Add the fresh and hard ciders, apple cider vinegar, salt, cinnamon, allspice, garlic, and ancho chilies. Increase the heat to high and bring to a full boil. Stir in the squash and reduce the heat to maintain a slow, steady simmer. Cover tightly and cook until the squash is tender, 20 minutes or so. Serve in festive bowls sprinkled with spicy roasted chickpeas and topped with spoonfuls of sage, pumpkin seed, and goat cheese pesto.

baked tomatoes, fennel, garlic, and feta

orecchiette, wilted spinach

There are many ways to enjoy this classic medley of Mediterranean flavours. In this version patience is the secret ingredient. Time spent slowly baking tomatoes, fennel, and garlic, gradually releasing and intensifying their sweet aromatic flavours. Time spent leisurely browning crumbly feta. Time spent waiting until the last second to wilt bright green spinach with freshly cooked pasta. Your reward awaits.

Preheat the oven to 350°F (180°C). Turn on the convection fan if you have one.

In a large bowl, toss together the tomatoes, fennel, garlic, chickpeas, olives, olive oil, fennel seeds, oregano, chili flakes, and salt. Transfer to a large ovenproof skillet or baking dish. Evenly crumble the feta over the top. Bake until bubbling and golden brown, an hour or so.

As the vegetables finish baking, bring a large pot of salted water to a full boil over high heat. Toss in the pasta and cook, stirring occasionally, until tender yet still slightly chewy, 12 minutes or so. Drain the pasta. Immediately add the baby spinach to the empty pot. Top with the drained pasta and stir together briefly. Cover tightly and rest for another minute or so, allowing the residual heat of the pasta to finish wilting the spinach. Serve topped with steaming spoonfuls of the baked tomatoes, fennel, garlic, and feta. Serve with lemon wedges.

Serves 6 as a vegetarian meal or 8 as a side

1 pound (450 g) assorted cherry, grape, or mini tomatoes

1 fennel bulb, trimmed, halved, cored, and thinly sliced lengthwise

Cloves from 2 heads of garlic, peeled and halved

1 can (19 ounces/540 g) chickpeas, drained and rinsed

1 cup (250 mL) Kalamata olives, pitted

2 tablespoons (30 mL) olive oil

1 tablespoon (15 mL) fennel seeds

1 teaspoon (5 mL) dried oregano

1 teaspoon (5 mL) Red Chili Flakes (page 219) or store-bought

½ teaspoon (2 mL) sea salt

1 pound (450 g) feta cheese

1 pound (450 g) orecchiette or your favourite pasta

10 ounces (280 g) baby spinach

1 lemon, cut into wedges

asparagus dill frittata

shaved asparagus salad

Serves 8 as a vegetarian meal

The gloriously herbaceous flavour of asparagus shines in many ways in this recipe: beautiful whole stalks on top, stems puréed into the frittata mixture, and tips stirred in for their tasty texture. Raw stalks are peeled into deliciously crisp shavings for a simple salad to round out this satisfying meal. Goat cheese adds its characteristic rich tang to the frittata, while fragrant dill brings complementary aromatic freshness.

Prep the Dill and Asparagus

Trim 2 inches (5 cm) of fronds from the dill and reserve for the salad. Thinly slice the remaining fronds and tender stems and reserve for the frittata.

Reserve 8 asparagus spears to top the frittata. Trim the bottom 2 inches (5 cm) from the remaining spears and reserve the pieces for the frittata batter. Place the trimmed asparagus spears on a work surface and, using a vegetable peeler, peel into long, thin strips, peeling from the base of the tip to the bottom of the spear. Transfer the shaved asparagus and the tips to a small bowl and reserve for the salad.

Make the Asparagus Dill Frittata

Preheat the oven to 350°F (180°C). Turn on the convection fan if you have one.

Combine the reserved asparagus pieces, ½ cup (125) of the milk, and 4 tablespoons (60 mL) of the butter in a small pot over medium heat. Bring to a simmer and cook until the asparagus is tender, 5 minutes or so. Transfer the works to a high-speed blender. Add the remaining ½ cup (125 mL) milk and the goat cheese and carefully purée until smooth. (Hot liquids are dangerous—they can violently erupt. For safety, drape a kitchen towel over the blender, start slowly, then gradually increase the speed.) In a large bowl, whisk the eggs together. Add the puréed asparagus mixture and whisk until smooth. Stir in the thinly sliced dill, salt, and pepper.

Melt the remaining 1 tablespoon (15 mL) butter in a large non-stick skillet over medium heat, swirling to evenly coat the pan. Remove from the heat. Pour in the egg mixture. Place the reserved 8 asparagus spears on top of the mixture, arranging them like spokes. Bake until the top is golden brown and the eggs are set, 20 to 25 minutes. Remove from the oven and rest for a few minutes before slicing.

Finish the Shaved Asparagus Salad

To the shaved asparagus and asparagus tips, add the reserved dill fronds and pickled red onions and juices. Gently toss together. Serve with sliced asparagus dill frittata.

Asparagus Dill Frittata

1 bunch of fresh dill

2 bunches of asparagus, woody ends trimmed

1 cup (250 mL) whole milk, divided

5 tablespoons (75 mL) butter, divided

4 ounces (115 g) soft goat cheese

12 eggs

1 teaspoon (5 mL) sea salt

Freshly ground pepper

Shaved Asparagus Salad

Reserved asparagus strips and tops (from Prep the Dill and Asparagus at left)

Reserved dill fronds (from Prep the Dill and Asparagus at left)

1 cup (250 mL) Pickled Red Onions and pickling juices (page 222)

cauliflower mac 'n' cheese
avonlea cheddar, caraway rye crust

You can mix an entire head of cauliflower into a batch of classic mac 'n' cheese. Puréeing half the head into the sauce as a thickener is the tasty secret. That's not the only upgrade, though. For richest flavour, use the very best cheddar, like Avonlea Cheddar, an exceptional cheese made the old-fashioned way by Cows Creamery on Prince Edward Island. Level up the crust, too, with rye bread for flavour and more cheese for crispy texture!

Make the Cauliflower Mac 'n' Cheese
Preheat the oven to 350°F (180°C). Turn on the convection fan if you have one.

Bring a large pot of salted water to a furious boil. Add the pasta and cook until tender yet still slightly chewy, 10 minutes or so. Drain the pasta and reserve. Rinse the pot.

Toss half the cauliflower florets and all the chopped stems into the pot. Add the milk and bring to a simmer over medium heat. Cover and cook until the cauliflower is tender, 10 minutes or so. Transfer the mixture to a high-speed blender. Add the garlic, mustard, paprika, and salt. Carefully purée until smooth. (Hot liquids are dangerous—they can violently erupt. For safety, drape a kitchen towel over the blender, start slowly, then gradually increase the speed.) Return the sauce to the pot. Whisk in the cheese until smooth. Stir in the pasta and remaining cauliflower florets. Transfer to a 13 x 9-inch (3.5 L) baking dish.

Make the Caraway Rye Crust and Bake
Toss the butter into a small saucepan over medium-high heat. Swirl gently as it melts, steams, foams, and eventually lightly browns. Remove from the heat and add the caraway seeds, swirling and gently toasting until fragrant, a minute or so. Break the bread into a food processor and pulse, grinding into rough crumbs. Add the butter mixture and the reserved 1 cup (250 mL) of cheese. Pulse just enough to mix into coarse crumbs. Spread into a thick, even layer over the mac 'n' cheese. Bake until golden brown and bubbly, about 45 minutes.

Serves 6 as a vegetarian meal or 12 as a side

Cauliflower Mac 'n' Cheese
2 cups (500 mL) elbow macaroni

1 head of cauliflower, cut into medium florets, stem chopped

2 cups (500 mL) whole milk

4 garlic cloves, thinly sliced

2 tablespoons (30 mL) Dijon mustard

1 tablespoon (15 mL) sweet paprika

1 teaspoon (5 mL) sea salt

1 pound (450 g) Avonlea Clothbound Cheddar (see page 229) or another aged cheddar cheese, coarsely grated, 1 cup (250 mL) reserved for the crust

Caraway Rye Crust
4 tablespoons (60 mL) butter

1 tablespoon (15 mL) caraway seeds

8 ounces (225 g) light rye bread

Reserved grated cheddar cheese (from above)

quinoa feta stuffed bell peppers
yellow tomato sauce

Mother Nature created hollow bell peppers for stuffing with goodness. Nutty protein-rich quinoa and rich, briny feta cheese combine to make an easily flavoured stuffing base. Poblano pepper, Kalamata olives, sun-dried tomatoes, and lots of fresh basil complete the package, but the sauce just might steal the show. Sunny-ripe tomatoes are so delicious they don't need to be cooked to make sauce. A simple purée is all it takes to show off their fragrant ripe flavours.

Make the Quinoa
Bring the water to a boil in a small saucepan over high heat. Stir in the quinoa and salt, cover, and reduce the heat to a slow, steady simmer. Cook until the quinoa is tender and fragrant, 15 minutes or so. Without uncovering, remove from the heat and let sit for 5 minutes.

Stuff and Bake the Bell Peppers
Preheat the oven to 375°F (190°C). Turn on the convection fan if you have one.

Cut the tops off the bell peppers and remove the seeds and membranes. Chop the edible part of the tops. Cut the stem off the poblano. Slice the poblano in half, remove the seeds, then roughly chop.

Heat the vegetable oil in a large, heavy sauté pan or non-stick skillet over medium-high heat. Add the bell pepper trimmings, poblano, onions, garlic, and fennel seeds and sauté until the peppers are soft and fragrant, 5 minutes or so. Remove from the heat. Stir in the cooked quinoa, olives, sun-dried tomatoes, basil, and half of the feta. Evenly and firmly stuff the bell peppers. Sprinkle the tops with the remaining feta. Transfer to a 13 x 9-inch (3.5 L) baking pan. Bake until the peppers are tender and the feta is lightly browned, 30 minutes or so.

Meanwhile, Make the Yellow Tomato Sauce
In a high-speed blender, combine the tomatoes, canola oil, lemon zest and juice, mustard, hot sauce, and salt. Purée until smooth. Use immediately or transfer to a resealable container and refrigerate for up to 3 days. Evenly pour the sauce into a pool on plates, nestle a quinoa feta stuffed pepper on top, and top with a basil sprig.

Serves 6 as a vegetarian meal or 8 as a side

Quinoa Feta Stuffed Bell Peppers

2 cups (500 mL) water

1 cup (250 mL) quinoa (any colour)

½ teaspoon (2 mL) sea salt

6 red bell peppers

1 poblano pepper

2 tablespoons (30 mL) vegetable oil

2 yellow onions, thinly sliced

6 garlic cloves, thinly sliced

1 tablespoon (15 mL) fennel seeds

1 cup (250 mL) Kalamata olives, pitted

1 cup (250 mL) drained oil-packed sun-dried tomatoes, thinly sliced

1 bunch of fresh basil, leaves tightly rolled and thinly sliced, a few sprigs reserved for garnish

1 block (14 ounces/400 g) feta cheese, drained and crumbled, divided

Yellow Tomato Sauce

2 or 3 large ripe yellow tomatoes or another heirloom varietal, quartered

¼ cup (60 mL) extra-virgin canola or olive oil

Zest and juice of 1 lemon

1 teaspoon (5 mL) Dijon mustard

½ teaspoon (2 mL) of your favourite hot sauce

½ teaspoon (2 mL) sea salt

soba noodle bowl with golden tofu, garden peas, cinnamon basil, and miso carrot broth

Serves 4 as a vegetarian meal or 8 as a side

We grow many types of garden peas and a wide variety of basils at the inn. When they're all at their sun-ripe peak they're delicious tossed together into a simple salad with a bright, tangy dressing. This meal in a bowl includes the nutty chewiness of soba noodles and golden-brown fried tofu in a fragrant savoury-sweet broth.

Pan-Fry the Golden Tofu
Wrap the block of tofu in several layers of paper towel. Press firmly to absorb the surface moisture. Unwrap the tofu and cut into 1-inch-thick (2.5 cm) slices. Stack the slices, a few at a time, and cut into large bite-size cubes.

Heat the vegetable oil in a large non-stick skillet over medium-high heat. Working in batches to avoid crowding the pan, fry the tofu cubes in a single layer, turning occasionally and adjusting the heat to maintain a steady sizzle, until evenly browned all over, 10 minutes or so. Transfer the tofu to layers of paper towel and let sit.

Cook the Soba Noodles
Bring a large pot of unsalted water to a full boil. Add the noodles and cook until nearly tender, 4 to 5 minutes. Drain in a colander and rinse well under cold running water, stirring gently with your hand until cool. Divide the noodles evenly among bowls.

Make the Miso Carrot Broth
In a small saucepan, combine the carrot juice, ginger, hot sauce, and lime zest and juice. Bring to a full simmer over medium heat. Remove from the heat. In a small bowl, whisk the miso with ¼ cup (60 mL) or so of the hot carrot juice. Whisk the slurry into the pot.

Finish the Soba Noodle Bowl
Lightly toss together the fried tofu, fresh peas, sugar snap peas, pea shoots, basil leaves, and preserved lemon dressing. Ladle the miso carrot broth over the soba noodles. Top with a handful of the pea basil salad.

Golden Tofu
1 block (12 ounces/340 g) firm or extra-firm tofu

¼ cup (60 mL) vegetable oil

Soba Noodle Bowl
12 ounces (340 g) dry soba noodles

1 pound (450 g) fresh peas, shucked (about 1 cup/250 mL)

8 ounces (225 g) sugar snap peas, snow peas, or other edible-pod pea variety, thinly sliced

A handful of pea shoots

Leaves from 1 large bunch of fresh cinnamon basil or other basil variety

¼ cup (60 mL) Preserved Lemon Dressing (page 220)

Miso Carrot Broth
4 cups (1 L) carrot juice

1 (2-inch/5 cm) piece frozen ginger, grated into a powder with a microplane

1 teaspoon (5 mL) of your favourite hot sauce

Zest and juice of 1 lime

¼ cup (60 mL) yellow miso

bok choy and edamame

ginger lime coconut broth, sweet potato jasmine rice

The secret to this meal in a bowl is simple: savoury greens wilt to tenderness in simmering broth. In this case, that means crisp, sweet baby bok choy and chewy edamame, quickly cooked in coconut milk brightly flavoured with ginger, lime, chili, and fish sauce. It's easy, too, to take the rice to the next level by stirring in the goodness of sweet potato. What a great way to eat your vegetables!

Toast the Coconut

Preheat the oven to 350°F (180°C). Line a baking sheet with parchment paper and spread the coconut evenly on it. Bake, stirring every 2 minutes, until evenly toasted and golden brown, 10 minutes or so.

Make the Sweet Potato Jasmine Rice

In a medium saucepan, combine the rice, sweet potato, water, salt, and bay leaf. Bring to a full simmer, stirring frequently, over medium-high heat. Reduce the heat to the lowest setting, cover tightly, and cook until the rice and sweet potato are tender, 20 minutes. Without uncovering, remove from the heat and let sit for 10 minutes.

Make the Ginger Lime Coconut Broth and Finish

Heat the vegetable oil in a large saucepan over medium heat. Add the shallots, ginger, and serrano pepper. Cook, stirring constantly, until fragrant but not browned, a minute or two. Add the coconut milk, lime zest and juice, and fish sauce. Bring to a steady simmer. Add the bok choy and edamame. Cook just until the leaves are bright green and wilted, 2 or 3 minutes.

Assemble the Bowls

Add a steaming spoonful of sweet potato jasmine rice to each bowl. Divide the bok choy and edamame evenly between the bowls. Ladle broth over the vegetables. Sprinkle with lots of toasted coconut.

Serves 4 as vegetarian meal or 8 as a side

Ginger Lime Coconut Broth

1 cup (250 mL) unsweetened shredded coconut

1 tablespoon (15 mL) vegetable oil

2 shallots, thinly sliced

1 (3-inch/8 cm) piece fresh ginger, peeled and cut into matchsticks

1 serrano or jalapeño pepper, stem and seeds removed, minced

2 cans (14 ounces/398 mL each) full-fat coconut milk

Zest and juice of 2 limes

1 tablespoon (15 mL) fish sauce

Sweet Potato Jasmine Rice

1 cup (250 mL) jasmine rice

1 sweet potato, peeled and coarsely shredded

1¼ cups (300 mL) water

½ teaspoon (2 mL) sea salt

1 bay leaf

Bok Choy and Edamame

4 heads baby bok choy, trimmed and leaves separated

2 cups (500 mL) shelled edamame (about 8 ounces/225 g)

mujadara and wilted kale

cumin browned onions, preserved lemon dressing

Mujadara is a staple of Arabic cooking and one of the world's great vegetarian staples. Lentils and rice. A legume, a grain. Together a complete source of protein. In this classic dish the lentils and rice come alive with Middle Eastern spices. A hearty greens salad of warm wilted kale tossed with bright, aromatic Preserved Lemon Dressing completes the meal.

Make the Cumin Browned Onions
Heat the vegetable oil in a small saucepan over medium heat. Sprinkle in the cumin seeds, gently shaking and briefly sizzling. Add the onions and salt. Slowly cook, stirring frequently, until browned, 20 minutes or so. Reduce the heat occasionally to prevent burning. Transfer to a small plate and reserve.

Make the Mujadara
Pour the vegetable oil into a large saucepan over medium heat. Add the onion and cook until soft and translucent, 5 minutes or so. Stir in the garlic, cumin, coriander, allspice, cinnamon, and ginger and cook briefly to release their full flavours, just 1 minute. Add the lentils, water, and salt. Bring to a boil, reduce the heat to a slow simmer, cover tightly, and cook for 12 minutes. Stir in the rice and raisins, cover, and continue cooking until the rice is tender and fluffy, 20 minutes more. Without uncovering, remove from the heat and let sit for 10 minutes.

Meanwhile, Make the Wilted Kale
Bring the water and salt to a full simmer in a large saucepan over medium heat. Stir in the kale, cover tightly, and cook just until the leaves are bright green and tender, 3 minutes or so. Drain well, then stir in the preserved lemon dressing.

To Serve
Spoon the mujadara onto individual plates or a large shared platter. Form a bed of wilted kale on individual plates or a large shared platter. Spoon the mujadara over the kale and top with cumin brown onions.

Serves 4 as a vegetarian meal or 8 as a side

Cumin Browned Onions

2 tablespoons (30 mL) vegetable oil

2 tablespoons (30 mL) cumin seeds

1 pound (450 g) yellow onions, thinly sliced

¼ teaspoon (1 mL) sea salt

Mujadara

2 tablespoons (30 mL) vegetable oil

1 large yellow onion, finely diced

4 garlic cloves, minced

1 teaspoon (5 mL) ground cumin

1 teaspoon (5 mL) ground coriander

½ teaspoon (2 mL) ground allspice

½ teaspoon (2 mL) cinnamon

½ teaspoon (2 mL) ground ginger

1 cup (250 mL) green lentils

4 cups (1 L) water

2 teaspoons (10 mL) sea salt

1 cup (250 mL) basmati rice

1 cup (250 mL) dark raisins

Wilted Kale

½ cup (125 mL) water

1 teaspoon (5 mL) sea salt

1 pound (450 g) kale, centre ribs removed, leaves cut into large pieces

¼ cup (60 mL) Preserved Lemon Dressing (page 220)

farmhouse vegetables

root vegetable pavé

rosemary beet purée, roast garlic labneh

Pavé is French for "cobblestone" and cheferly for flat, rectangular food often composed of many layers. The elaborate method wonderfully highlights the distinctive flavours of earthy root vegetables. This dish may be served directly from the oven, but for show-stopping presentation it's best to refrigerate it overnight until firm. Then it's easy to cut into precise shapes and reheat.

Slow roasting (or baking) removes the sharp pungency from garlic, allowing its natural sweetness and mellow fragrance to emerge. Whisk into rich yogurt with bright lemon and drain overnight to concentrate those flavours into thick, tangy labneh.

Serves 4 as a vegetable main or 12 as a side

Roast Garlic Labneh (makes about 1½ cups/375 mL)

2 heads of garlic

2 teaspoons (10 mL) olive oil

1 cup (250 mL) natural plain full-fat yogurt or plain Greek yogurt

1 teaspoon (5 mL) Preserved Lemon Purée (page 221) (or the zest and juice of 1 lemon and ½ teaspoon/ 2 mL sea salt)

¼ teaspoon (1 mL) Red Chili Flakes (page 219) or store-bought

Root Vegetable Pavé

1 pound (450 g) baking potatoes (2 or 3 large potatoes), peeled

1 cup (250 mL) extra-virgin canola or olive oil, divided

Leaves and tender stems from 1 bunch of fresh thyme, finely minced (2 tablespoons/30 mL or so), divided

Sea salt

Freshly ground pepper

1 pound (450 g) carrots (3 or 4 large carrots), peeled

1 pound (450 g) parsnips (3 or 4 parsnips), peeled

1 large turnip (1 pound/450 g), peeled

1 pound (450 g) sweet potatoes (2 potatoes), peeled

1 large celery root (1 pound/450 g), peeled and rinsed

Rosemary Beet Purée

1 pound (450 g) red beets

¼ cup (60 mL) red wine vinegar

Leaves and tender stems from 1 sprig of fresh rosemary, minced

2 tablespoons (30 mL) extra-virgin canola or olive oil

½ teaspoon (2 mL) sea salt

¼ teaspoon (1 mL) Red Chili Flakes (page 219) or store-bought

Make the Roast Garlic Labneh

Preheat the oven to 375°F (190°C). Turn on the convection fan if you have one.

Slice off the top third of the garlic heads with a serrated knife to expose the cloves. Place the garlic heads on a small baking sheet. Drizzle the exposed cloves with the olive oil. Bake until the cloves soften, begin oozing, and lightly brown, 45 minutes or so. Remove from the oven and let sit until cool enough to handle. Carefully squeeze the garlic cloves out of their skins and into a small bowl. Whisk in the yogurt, preserved lemon purée, and chili flakes. Transfer to a strainer lined with folded cheesecloth suspended over a small bowl. Cover completely with plastic wrap, refrigerate, and let drain for 24 hours. Discard the whey. Reserve or transfer to a resealable container and refrigerate for up to 5 days.

Make the Root Vegetable Pavé

Preheat the oven to 350°F (180°C). Turn on the convection fan if you have one. Lightly oil a 13 x 9-inch (3.5 L) baking dish and line the bottom with a piece of precisely fitted parchment paper.

Gather and prep the root vegetables. Using a mandoline, slice the potatoes lengthwise as thinly as possible. Form a stack or two with some of the larger slices and cut in half lengthwise to form straight edges. Transfer all the slices to a medium bowl, add 1 teaspoon (5 mL) of the canola oil and 1 teaspoon (5 mL) of the minced thyme, season lightly with salt and pepper, and gently toss. Make a thin, even layer of potato slices in the bottom of the dish, fitting the straight edges to the sides of the dish and filling the centre with the remaining slices. Continue layering as evenly and precisely as possible with the remaining potato slices, pressing firmly as you go.

Continue forming distinct layers of each root vegetable in succession, slicing lengthwise carrots, parsnips, turnip, sweet potatoes, and lastly celery root, and tossing each with canola oil, thyme, and salt and pepper before layering and pressing. Seal tightly with foil. Cover with a baking sheet to weigh down and fully seal the edges. Bake until tender, 2 hours or so. Serve immediately from the pan, or for full presentation continue with the steps below.

Press and Refrigerate the Root Vegetable Pavé

Remove the foil and place a layer of plastic wrap or parchment paper directly on the pavé's surface. Top with a second baking dish that fits just inside the baking dish (or cut a piece of cardboard to fit and wrap it in foil), and using your hands lightly press the layers together. Refrigerate overnight with the dish weighing down the pavé.

recipe continues

Make the Rosemary Beet Purée

Trim the stems from the red beets. Wearing gloves to minimize staining, peel the beets. Using a juicer, juice half of the beets until you have ½ cup (125 mL) of juice. Discard the pulp. Quarter the remaining beets. Transfer the beets and juice to a small saucepan and add the red wine vinegar and rosemary. Bring to a simmer over medium-high heat. Cover tightly, adjust the heat, and slowly simmer until tender, 15 minutes or so. Transfer the works to a high-speed blender. Add the canola oil, salt, and chili flakes. Purée until silky smooth. Taste and adjust seasoning. Reserve or transfer to a resealable container and refrigerate for up to 3 days.

To Serve the Root Vegetable Pavé

Preheat the oven to 425°F (220°C). Turn on the convection fan if you have one. Line a baking sheet with a silicone baking mat or parchment paper.

Release the pavé from the baking dish by running a thin knife between it and the pan's edge. Top with a baking sheet and carefully invert so the pavé is on the bottom of the sheet. Lift away the baking dish and peel away the parchment paper. Cut the pavé into even rectangles (6 large or 12 smaller) and place on the prepared baking sheet. Bake until heated through, 15 minutes or so. Alternatively, reheat in the microwave. Serve with rosemary beet purée and roast garlic labneh.

root vegetable chowder

whey, cream, butter

The humble earthy flavours of root vegetables fill this chowder with rich depth. Leftover whey from cheesemaking is an excellent neutral simmering base, and cream adds finishing richness. The potatoes dissolve and thicken the broth while the other root vegetables remain distinct. Bright herbs, melting in a pool of lemony butter, add aromatic complexity.

Make the Herb Butter

In a small bowl, mash together the butter, herbs, and lemon zest and juice. Reserve, or let sit at room temperature for a few hours, or transfer to a resealable container and refrigerate for up to 3 days. Bring to room temperature before using.

Make the Root Vegetable Chowder

Melt the butter in a large soup pot or Dutch oven over medium heat. Add the onions, cover, and cook, stirring frequently, until softened and golden brown, 10 minutes or so. Add the garlic, stirring until fragrant, a minute or so. Add the carrots, potatoes, turnip, whey, and bay leaves. Bring to a simmer, cover, and cook for 10 minutes. Add the parsnips and celery root, cover, and continue cooking until all the vegetables are tender and the potato has dissolved and thickened the chowder. Stir in the cream, salt, and pepper. Return to a simmer. Serve with dollops of herb butter melting and pooling on the surface of the chowder.

Serves 4 as a vegetable main or 8 as a side with leftover herb butter

Herb Butter

½ cup (125 mL) butter, softened

¼ cup (60 mL) finely chopped fresh herb leaves and tender stems (one or a few varieties: tarragon, lovage, thyme, sage, rosemary, chives, sorrel, dill, chervil, parsley)

Zest and juice of 1 lemon

Root Vegetable Chowder

4 tablespoons (60 mL) butter

2 yellow onions, finely diced

4 garlic cloves, finely minced

2 carrots, peeled and diced

2 large baking potatoes, washed and diced

1 turnip, peeled and diced

4 cups (1 L) whey, whole milk, Vegetable Broth (page 34), or water

2 bay leaves

2 or 3 parsnips (about 1 pound/450 g), peeled and diced

1 celery root (about 1 pound/ 450 g), peeled, rinsed, and diced

1 cup (250 mL) heavy (35%) cream

1 teaspoon (5 mL) sea salt

Freshly ground pepper

whole roasted celery root

celery lovage slaw, lovage oil

The sweet, floral fragrance and subtle bitterness of celery runs deep in this dish. Mellow flavour emerges from celery root through slow, patient roasting. It's also delicious raw in a traditional slaw alongside its above-ground cousin, crisp celery stalks. Lovage is another intensely aromatic member of the family, with a distinctive celery flavour of its own. The family of celery flavours is balanced by a bright, tangy dressing.

Make the Lovage Oil

Bring a small saucepan of salted water to a boil over medium-high heat. Toss in the lovage and cook, stirring, just until it brightens, a minute at most. Drain the lovage and press out the water. In a blender, purée the lovage leaves with the vegetable oil until smooth and green. Return to the pot and, stirring occasionally, quickly bring to a full simmer over medium heat. Immediately pour into a fine-mesh sieve positioned over a bowl. Strain, without pressing, until fully drained, an hour or so. Reserve or transfer to a resealable container and refrigerate for up to 3 days. Bring to room temperature when ready to use.

Make the Celery Lovage Slaw

In a medium bowl, combine the mayonnaise, apple cider vinegar, mustard, honey, hot sauce, celery seeds, and salt. Whisk into a smooth dressing. Stir in the celery root, celery stalks, dill pickle, lovage leaves, and green onions, evenly coating with dressing. Reserve or transfer to a resealable container and refrigerate for up to 3 days.

Roast the Celery Root

Preheat the oven to 350°F (180°C). Turn on the convection fan if you have one.

Evenly rub each whole celery root with the vegetable oil and pierce 20 times all over with the tip of a small sharp knife. Place on a baking sheet or in a shallow baking pan and roast until tender, at least 2 hours. Watch for oozing, browning juices, a sign that the root is cooked through and tender. Use immediately or rest until cool. Quarter into wedges, lightly season with salt and pepper, and drizzle with lovage oil. Form a bed of celery lovage slaw on individual plates or a large shared platter. Top with roasted celery root wedges and reserved celery leaves.

Serves 4 as a vegetable main or 8 as a side with extra lovage oil

Lovage Oil (makes 1 cup/ 250 mL)

A handful of fresh lovage leaves (about 1 cup/250 mL)

1 cup (250 mL) vegetable oil

Celery Lovage Slaw

¼ cup (60 mL) mayonnaise

2 tablespoons (30 mL) apple cider vinegar

1 tablespoon (15 mL) yellow or Dijon mustard

1 tablespoon (15 mL) pure liquid honey

1 teaspoon (5 mL) of your favourite hot sauce

1 teaspoon (5 mL) celery seeds

½ teaspoon (2 mL) sea salt

1 celery root (1 pound/450 g), peeled, rinsed, and coarsely grated

2 celery stalks, tender leaves minced and reserved, stalks cut diagonally into thin slivers

1 large dill pickle, minced

12 fresh lovage leaves, stacked, tightly rolled, and very thinly sliced

4 green onions, cut diagonally into thin slivers

Whole Roasted Celery Root

2 celery roots (1 pound/450 g each), unpeeled, hairy roots trimmed, scrubbed clean, rinsed, and dried

¼ cup (60 mL) vegetable oil or reserved animal fat (see page 3)

Sea salt

Freshly ground pepper

whole roasted turnip

cranberry rosemary chutney

Serves 4 as a vegetable main or 8 as a side

Whole vegetables can be tasty when roasted like meat. Turnips have a rich and mellow flavour that only emerges after patient roasting. Given time, the tough root's durable flesh eventually relaxes into a juicy textural treat, ready for a contrasting condiment. Here, fragrant rosemary and woodsy juniper aromatize bright, balanced cranberry chutney.

Make the Cranberry Rosemary Chutney

In a small saucepan, combine the cranberries, apple, apple cider, apple cider vinegar, brown sugar, rosemary, chili flakes, juniper, allspice, and salt. Bring to a simmer over medium heat and cook, stirring occasionally, until the fruit is tender and the chutney has thickened a bit, 15 minutes or so. Remove from the heat. Let sit until cool and further thickened, or transfer to a resealable container and refrigerate for up to 3 days.

Roast the Turnips

Preheat the oven to 350°F (180°C). Turn on the convection fan if you have one. Line a baking sheet with a silicone baking mat or parchment paper.

Evenly rub the turnips with the vegetable oil and salt. Place the turnips on the prepared baking sheet and roast until tender and fragrant, 2 hours or so. Remove from the oven and rest until cool enough to handle. Cut into wedges and serve with the cranberry rosemary chutney.

Cranberry Rosemary Chutney

2 cups (500 mL) fresh or frozen cranberries

1 large crisp apple (Honeycrisp, Gala, Cortland, McIntosh), unpeeled, cored and diced

1 cup (250 mL) fresh apple cider

¼ cup (60 mL) apple cider vinegar

½ cup (125 mL) tightly packed brown sugar

Leaves from 1 sprig of fresh rosemary, minced

1 teaspoon (5 mL) Red Chili Flakes (page 219) or store-bought

1 teaspoon (5 mL) ground juniper berries

½ teaspoon (2 mL) ground allspice

1 teaspoon (5 mL) sea salt

Whole Roasted Turnip

2 large turnips (about 2 pounds/900 g total), scrubbed

1 tablespoon (15 mL) vegetable oil

1 teaspoon (5 mL) sea salt

roasted beets

mint labneh

The sweet, earthy flavour of beets deepens through roasting. Roasted beets are particularly delicious served with any rich, creamy topping like sour cream, fresh cheese (page 225), or Middle Eastern labneh (drained full-fat yogurt). It's easy to make your own labneh with lots of fresh mint for bright contrast.

Make the Mint Labneh

Purée the yogurt, mint, and salt in a food processor. Transfer to a strainer lined with folded cheesecloth suspended over a medium bowl. Cover completely with plastic wrap, refrigerate, and let drain for 24 hours. Discard the whey. Reserve or transfer to a resealable container and refrigerate for up to 3 days.

Roast the Beets

Preheat the oven to 425°F (220°C). Turn on the convection fan if you have one.

Trim the stems from the beets. Cut into quarters. Toss the beet wedges with the vegetable oil, salt, and pepper. Transfer to a 13 x 9-inch (3.5 L) baking dish. Pour in the water and cover tightly with foil. Bake until tender, 30 minutes or so. Remove the foil and continue baking, gently shaking the dish occasionally, until the water has evaporated and the beets are lightly caramelized, 15 minutes or so more. Serve hot or at room temperature with spoonfuls of mint labneh.

Serves 4 to 6 as a vegetable side

Mint Labneh

2 cups (500 mL) natural plain full-fat yogurt or plain Greek yogurt

20 fresh mint leaves (from 2 or 3 sprigs)

½ teaspoon (2 mL) sea salt

Roasted Beets

2 pounds (900 g) red, yellow, or heirloom beets

2 tablespoons (30 mL) vegetable oil

1 teaspoon (5 mL) sea salt

Lots of freshly ground pepper

¼ cup (60 mL) water

grilled carrots
carrot horseradish jam

Grilled carrots are sublime. Somehow they have the ability to char without tasting burnt. With searing heat and patient tending, their interior tenderizes while their exterior flavourfully caramelizes. Medium carrots work best; larger ones will burn long before they cook through. The sweet earthiness of carrots also stars in an intriguing condiment made by simmering them in their own juice.

Make the Carrot Horseradish Jam
Using a juicer, juice about half the orange carrots until you have 1 cup (250 mL) of juice. Peel and shred the remaining carrots. Combine the shredded carrots, carrot juice, honey, and salt in a medium saucepan. Cook over medium heat, stirring frequently, until the carrots soften and the juice reduces by half, 10 minutes or so. Transfer the mixture to a food processor, add the horseradish and tarragon, and purée until smooth. Reserve or transfer to a resealable container and refrigerate for up to 3 days.

Grill the Carrots
Build and tend an aromatic fire in your firepit, burning down to a thick bed of glowing hot coals. Alternatively, fire up your barbecue or grill.

Lightly rub the carrots with the vegetable oil, salt, and pepper. Grill, turning frequently, until tender and lightly charred, 15 minutes or so. Serve with the carrot horseradish jam.

Carrot Horseradish Jam

2 pounds (900 g) orange carrots, unpeeled

¼ cup (60 mL) pure liquid honey

½ teaspoon (2 mL) sea salt

¼ cup (60 mL) prepared horseradish

Leaves from a handful of fresh tarragon sprigs

Grilled Carrots

2 pounds (900 kg) various heirloom carrots, trimmed, peeled, and cut in half lengthwise

2 tablespoons (30 mL) vegetable oil

Sea salt

Lots of freshly ground pepper

grilled parsnips
parsley chimichurri

Parsnips are a relatively tender root vegetable, so they're easily grilled. Their exterior lightly chars while their interior cooks, the inside finishing before the outside burns. Their sweet, earthy flavours are complemented by the bright, bold flavours of a classic chimichurri—the all-purpose grilling condiment of Argentinean cuisine.

Make the Parsley Chimichurri
Whisk together the canola oil and red wine vinegar in a small bowl. Stir in the garlic, oregano, paprika, cumin, chili flakes, and salt. Stir in the parsley and green onions. To give the flavours time to fully develop, transfer to a resealable container and rest at room temperature for an hour or two or refrigerate for up to 5 days.

Grill the Parsnips
Build and tend an aromatic fire in your firepit, burning down to a thick bed of glowing hot coals. Alternatively, fire up your barbecue or grill.

Lightly rub the parsnips with the vegetable oil, salt, and pepper. Grill, turning frequently, until tender and lightly charred, 15 minutes or so. Serve with spoonfuls of the parsley chimichurri.

Serves 4 to 6 as a vegetable side with leftover parsley chimichurri

Parsley Chimichurri (makes about 2 cups/500 mL)

1 cup (250 mL) extra-virgin canola or olive oil

1 cup (250 mL) red wine vinegar

4 garlic cloves, finely grated with a microplane or finely minced

1 tablespoon (15 mL) dried oregano

1 teaspoon (5 mL) smoked paprika

1 teaspoon (5 mL) ground cumin

1 teaspoon (5 mL) Red Chili Flakes (page 219) or store-bought

1 teaspoon (5 mL) sea salt

1 bunch of fresh flat-leaf parsley, finely chopped (about ½ cup/125 mL)

4 green onions, thinly sliced

Grilled Parsnips

2 pounds (900 g) parsnips, trimmed, peeled, and cut in half lengthwise

1 tablespoon (15 mL) vegetable oil

1 teaspoon (5 mL) sea salt

Lots of freshly ground pepper

potato turnip mash

rosemary maple brown butter

Serves 4 to 6 as a vegetable side

The neutral earthy flavours of potatoes and turnips pair beautifully in this easy mash. Giving the much harder turnips a head start on the softer potatoes means they'll arrive together at the tender finish line. Plenty of time to perfume brown butter with fragrant rosemary, then sweeten it with maple.

Boil the Turnip and Potatoes

Bring a large pot of salted water to a full boil over medium-high heat. Add the turnip and bay leaves and cook for 10 minutes. Add the potatoes and cook until tender, 15 minutes or so. Meanwhile, in a small saucepan over medium heat, warm the milk and butter until gently simmering.

Make the Rosemary Maple Brown Butter

Toss the butter into a small saucepan over medium-high heat. Swirl gently as it melts, steams, foams, and eventually lightly browns. Swirl in the rosemary. Remove from the heat and let sit for a few minutes, allowing the flavours to emerge, before whisking in the maple syrup. Reserve.

Mash the Turnip and Potatoes

Drain the cooked turnips and potatoes. Return to the pot. Add the warm milk and salt. Mash as coarsely or smoothly as you like. Stir in the chives, reserving a few to sprinkle on top. Serve drizzled with the rosemary maple brown butter.

Potato Turnip Mash

1 large turnip (2 pounds/900 g), peeled, halved, and each half quartered

2 bay leaves

2 pounds (900 g) yellow or baking potatoes (4 to 6 large potatoes), peeled and quartered

1 cup (250 mL) whole milk

½ cup (125 mL) butter

1 teaspoon (5 mL) sea salt

1 bunch of fresh chives, thinly sliced

Rosemary Maple Brown Butter

4 tablespoons (60 mL) butter

Leaves from 1 sprig of fresh rosemary, minced

¼ cup (60 mL) pure maple syrup

cracked potatoes

sage brown butter

Makes 4 vegetable sides

It's hard to improve upon the perfection of a simple baked potato, but lots of butter just might be the way. A steaming baked potato, cracked open, basted with butter, baked even more until golden brown and crispy. But why stop there? Brown more butter, add the pungency of garlic, steep with the subtle fragrance of sage, and deliciously drizzle.

Preheat the oven to 425°F (220°C). Turn on the convection fan if you have one.

Bake the potatoes on a small baking sheet until tender, about 1 hour. Remove from the oven. Firmly press each potato with a large spatula, the back of a plate, or a small pan, lightly crushing and cracking open. Melt ¼ cup (60 mL) of the butter in a small skillet over medium-high heat. Drizzle evenly over the cracked potatoes. Return to the oven and bake until crispy golden brown, 20 minutes or so.

Toss the remaining ¼ cup (60 mL) butter into the skillet over medium-high heat, swirling gently as it melts, steams, foams, and eventually lightly browns. Remove from the heat and immediately stir in the sage and garlic. Count to 10, then add the lemon zest and juice, swirling to evenly combine.

Lightly season the potatoes with salt and pepper. Drizzle with the sage brown butter.

4 large baking potatoes (about 2 pounds/900 g), scrubbed

½ cup (125 mL) butter, divided

4 large sage leaves

2 garlic cloves, finely grated with a microplane or finely minced

Zest and juice of 1 lemon

Sea salt

Freshly ground pepper

potato gnocchi, nutmeg spinach sauce, and orach salad

Gnocchi are easily made deliciously chewy dumplings that are part mashed potato, part pasta. They're particularly tasty simply browned and crisped in butter. Tender spinach is puréed into a bright green sauce scented with fragrant nutmeg. Orach is an ancient vegetable with a savoury mineral flavour like spinach and chard. Its microgreens and tender leaves pair beautifully with earthy potatoes.

Make the Nutmeg Spinach Sauce

Melt the butter in a medium saucepan over medium heat. Stir in the onion, cover, and cook, stirring frequently, until soft and fragrant but not browning, 10 minutes or so. Stir in the garlic, nutmeg, salt, and pepper and continue cooking for a minute. Add the water and spinach and cook, stirring constantly, just until bright green and wilted, only a minute or two. Transfer to a high-speed blender and carefully purée until smooth. (Hot liquids are dangerous—they can violently erupt. For safety, drape a kitchen towel over the blender, start slowly, then gradually increase the speed.) Return the sauce to the pot and reserve at room temperature. Bring to a simmer just before serving.

Make the Potato Gnocchi

Place the potatoes in a large pot and cover with salted water. Bring to a boil over medium-high heat and cook until tender, 15 minutes or so. Drain the potatoes, rinse the pot, fill with hot water, and return to a simmer. Pass the potatoes through a ricer or food mill fitted with its finest disc into a large bowl and let cool until no longer steaming, 15 minutes or so. Sprinkle in 1½ cups (375 mL) of the flour. Add the eggs, salt, and pepper. With a sturdy wooden spoon, vigorously stir the mixture into a rough dough.

Measure the remaining ½ cup (125 mL) flour onto a work surface. Lightly flour your hands, reserving some flour to the side. Turn out the dough and lightly sprinkle with some of the reserved flour. Knead for a minute until a smooth dough emerges. Divide the dough into 4 equal pieces. Dust 1 piece of dough with flour and roll into a long, even rope about 1 inch (2.5 cm) thick. Repeat with the remaining 3 pieces. Cut each rope into 1-inch (2.5 cm) pieces. You should have 32 or so gnocchi.

recipe continues

Serves 4 as a vegetable main or 6 as a side

Nutmeg Spinach Sauce

2 tablespoons (30 mL) butter

1 yellow onion, diced

4 garlic cloves, finely grated with a microplane or finely minced

½ teaspoon (2 mL) ground nutmeg

½ teaspoon (2 mL) sea salt

Freshly ground pepper

½ cup (125 mL) water

10 ounces (280 g) baby spinach

Potato Gnocchi

4 large russet or Yukon Gold potatoes (about 2 pounds/ 900 g), peeled and quartered

2 cups (500 mL) all-purpose flour, divided

2 eggs, whisked

1 teaspoon (5 mL) sea salt

Freshly ground pepper

4 tablespoons (60 mL) butter

Salad Tangle

A handful of fresh orach leaves or baby spinach (2 ounces/ 57 g or so)

A handful of orach sprouts or other savoury, snappy fresh microgreens (broccoli, kale, radish, turnip, or cress; see page 229)

Bring the simmering water to a boil over medium-high heat. Working quickly, immediately transfer the gnocchi to the boiling water. Cook, stirring gently, until all the gnocchi are floating and cooked through, 3 to 4 minutes. Remove from the heat.

Melt the butter in a large non-stick skillet over medium-high heat. With a skimmer or slotted spoon, lift the cooked gnocchi from the water, draining thoroughly, and transfer to the melted butter. Without stirring, patiently cook the gnocchi until just one side is thoroughly browned and crispy. Serve on a pool of warm spinach sauce with a tangle of fresh orach leaves and orach sprouts.

cumin corn fritters, fresh pea mash, and purslane

ancho squeeze

Crisp corn fritters marry beautifully with gently mashed sweet peas with fragrant cumin seeds, spicy chili sauce, and a crisp, cool herb. Purslane is a juicy, tender leafy green vegetable and nutritional powerhouse that can be eaten raw or cooked. On many farms it's considered a weed and always seems to grow wild where you don't want it to. We try to train ours to stay in one spot because once corralled, this crisp, slightly salty yet sweet succulent is a welcome addition to any salad. An ancho is a dried medium-heat poblano pepper, and here it's easily simmered into a simple hot sauce.

Make the Ancho Squeeze

In a small saucepan, bring the chilies and tomato juice to a full simmer over medium heat. Cover tightly, remove from the heat, and rest until softened, 15 minutes. Transfer to a high-speed blender. Add the lime zest and juice, canola oil, mustard, and salt. Purée until smooth. Transfer to a squeeze bottle and reserve or refrigerate for up to 7 days.

Make the Cumin Corn Fritter Batter

Splash the corn oil into a small saucepan over medium heat. Add the cumin seeds and shake lightly until fragrant and toasted, just a minute or so. Add 1 cup (250 mL) of the corn kernels and the water. Bring to a simmer, cover, and cook just until the corn is tender, another minute or two. Transfer to a food processor, add the butter, and purée until smooth. Add the chickpea flour, salt, and baking soda. Process until thoroughly mixed. Add the remaining 1 cup (250 mL) corn kernels and pulse briefly, just enough to combine. Reserve or transfer to a resealable container and refrigerate for up to 3 days.

Fry the Cumin Corn Fritters

Heat the vegetable oil in a large pot or deep-fryer over medium-high heat until it reaches 375°F (190°C) on a deep-fat thermometer. Using 2 spoons, the first to scoop, the second to release the batter, gently drop spoonfuls of the batter into the hot oil. Work in batches so you don't crowd the pot. Adjust the heat to maintain the ideal frying temperature of 365°F (185°C). Fry, stirring gently with a skimmer or slotted spoon, until golden brown and crispy, 2 to 3 minutes. Drain briefly on paper towel. Lightly season with salt. (Cool, strain, and refrigerate the frying oil so you can use it again.)

recipe continues

Makes 12 or so fritters, enough for 4 to 6 as a vegetable side

Ancho Squeeze

4 dried ancho chilies, stems and seeds removed, cracked into small pieces

2 cups (500 mL) tomato juice or tomato purée

Zest and juice of 2 limes

2 tablespoons (30 mL) extra-virgin canola or olive oil

1 teaspoon (5 mL) mustard (yellow, Dijon, or grainy)

½ teaspoon (2 mL) sea salt

Cumin Corn Fritters

1 tablespoon (15 mL) corn oil or other vegetable oil

1 tablespoon (15 mL) cumin seeds

2 cups (500 mL) corn kernels (from 4 ears of fresh corn), divided

¾ cup (175 mL) water

4 tablespoons (60 mL) butter, softened or melted

2 cups (500 mL) chickpea flour

1 teaspoon (5 mL) sea salt

¼ teaspoon (1 mL) baking soda

4 cups (1 L) vegetable oil, for frying

Fresh Pea Mash and Purslane

2 pounds (900 g) fresh peas, shucked (2 cups/500 mL)

½ cup (125 mL) water

2 tablespoons (30 mL) butter or extra-virgin canola or olive oil

½ teaspoon (2 mL) sea salt

A handful or two of fresh purslane sprigs (about 4 ounces/115 g), washed and dried, for garnish

Mash the Fresh Peas

Combine the peas, water, butter, and salt in a small saucepan. Bring to a simmer over medium heat and cook just until the peas are bright green and tender, 3 minutes or so. Remove from the heat and mash with a potato masher or the back of a large spoon.

Serve the mashed peas immediately, topped with a pile of crisp cumin corn fritters, sprinkled with purslane, and decorated with ancho squeeze.

fried sunchokes

mushroom ketchup

Sunchokes were grown in the Indigenous kitchen gardens of Prince Edward Island, and foraged wild mushrooms were prized long before European cooks arrived. Today we also revere the fried tubers for their special flavour and textural balance, the perfect harmony of a crispy-crunchy outside and a smooth, creamy inside. Ketchup was classically made with mushrooms and other vegetables before tomatoes were discovered in the New World. This deeply flavoured condiment shows the affinity savoury mushrooms have with aromatic spices.

Make the Mushroom Ketchup

Combine the mushrooms and salt in a food processor and pulse just enough to finely chop and evenly mix but not enough to fully purée. Transfer to a large fine-mesh strainer, colander, or steamer basket positioned over a pot. Cover completely with plastic wrap. Refrigerate 1 full day to thoroughly drain the wet paste. Discard the salty liquid.

In a large saucepan, combine the mushroom paste with red wine vinegar, honey, garlic, pepper, ginger, nutmeg, allspice, and cloves. Bring to a full boil over medium heat, then reduce the heat to a slow, steady simmer. Cook, uncovered, stirring frequently, until reduced and thickened, 30 minutes or so. Serve warm, or transfer to a resealable container and refrigerate until cool. Refrigerate leftovers for up to 1 week.

Deep-Fry the Sunchokes

Heat the frying fat in a large pot or deep-fryer over medium-high heat until it reaches 375°F (190°C) on a deep-fat thermometer. Carefully add half of the sunchokes, talking care not to crowd the hot oil and lower its temperature too far. Adjust the heat to maintain the ideal frying temperature of 365°F (185°C). Fry, stirring gently with a skimmer or slotted spoon, until golden brown and crispy, 5 minutes or so. Drain on paper towel. Season generously with salt and pepper. Repeat with the remaining sunchokes. Serve with the mushroom ketchup for dipping. (Cool, strain, and refrigerate the frying fat so you can use it again.)

Mushroom Ketchup (makes 2 cups/500 mL)

2 pounds (900 g) brown cremini mushrooms, rinsed and drained

¼ cup (60 mL) sea salt

¼ cup (60 mL) red wine vinegar

¼ cup (60 mL) pure liquid honey

4 garlic cloves, finely grated with a microplane or finely minced

1 teaspoon (5 mL) freshly ground pepper

1 teaspoon (5 mL) ground ginger

1 teaspoon (5 mL) ground nutmeg

¼ teaspoon (1 mL) ground allspice

¼ teaspoon (1 mL) ground cloves

Fried Sunchokes

8 cups (2 L) lard, peanut oil, grapeseed oil, or rendered duck fat, for deep-frying

2 to 3 pounds (900 g to 1.35 kg) sunchokes, washed, well drained, and halved lengthwise

Sea salt

Lots of freshly ground pepper

cider-braised baby leeks

warm apple vinaigrette, crispy leeks

Serves 4 to 6 as a vegetable side

Leeks are the sweetest, mellowest members of the onion family and typically used merely to season other dishes. Here, though, they're front and centre. The elongated onion stalks softly melt in flavourful simmering cider. At the other end of the texture spectrum, crispy fried leeks add tasty contrast. Baby leeks are prized for their user-friendly size and tender sweetness. Larger leeks have more texture and just as much flavour.

Make the Crispy Leeks

Heat the vegetable oil in a large pot or deep-fryer over medium-high heat until it reaches 375°F (190°C) on a deep-fat thermometer. Carefully add the leeks to the hot oil and fry, stirring constantly with a skimmer or slotted spoon, until golden brown and crispy, just 1 to 2 minutes. Adjust the heat to maintain the ideal frying temperature of 365°F (185°C). Drain on paper towel. Lightly season with salt and pepper. (Cool, strain, and refrigerate the frying oil so you can use it again.)

Make the Cider-Braised Baby Leeks and Warm Apple Vinaigrette

Heat the vegetable oil in a large, heavy skillet over medium-high heat. Add the leeks and, without turning them, sear until golden brown on one side. Season with salt and pepper. Add the cider, then reduce the heat to a slow, steady simmer, cover tightly, and cook until very tender when pierced with a knife, 10 to 15 minutes, depending on size. Transfer to a serving platter, leaving the juices behind. Add the apple, increase the heat, and continue simmering, stirring constantly, until reduced and thickened. Remove from the heat. Whisk in the apple cider vinegar, mustard, and chives. Pour the warm apple vinaigrette over the braised leeks. Top with crispy leeks.

Crispy Leeks

4 cups (1 L) vegetable oil, for frying

2 or 3 baby leeks (or 1 large leek), trimmed, halved lengthwise, cleaned, cut into 3-inch (8 cm) sections, and sliced into very thin strips

Sea salt

Freshly ground pepper

Cider-Braised Baby Leeks and Warm Apple Vinaigrette

2 tablespoons (30 mL) vegetable oil

12 baby leeks, trimmed and cleaned (or 4 large leeks, trimmed, halved lengthwise, and cleaned)

Sea salt

Freshly ground pepper

12 ounces (340 g) Double Hill Nomad Cider (see page 229) or your favourite hard cider (or 1 cup/250 mL fresh apple cider or apple juice and ½ cup/125 mL white wine)

1 large tart apple (Honeycrisp, McIntosh, Cortland, or Gala), unpeeled, cored, and diced

1 tablespoon (15 mL) apple cider vinegar

1 teaspoon (5 mL) Dijon mustard

1 bunch of fresh chives, thinly sliced

whole roasted onions, grilled garlic scapes, and chive flowers

nutmeg soubise, crispy shallots

We grow many members of the onion family every year. This spectacular homage to these kitchen staples showcases humble onions slowly baked until tender and sweet; grilled garlic scapes, the plant's flower stalk, sharp, peppery, and deliciously tender; shallots crisply fried into mini onion rings; fragrant chive flowers; and creamy sauce soubise, classically thickened with onions.

Fry the Shallots

Heat the vegetable oil in a large pot or deep-fryer over medium-high heat until it reaches 375°F (190°C). In a small bowl toss together the shallots, cornstarch, and salt. Carefully add the shallots to the hot oil and fry, stirring constantly with a skimmer or slotted spoon, until golden brown and crispy, just 1 to 2 minutes. Drain on paper towel. Season with salt and pepper. (Cool, strain, and refrigerate the frying oil so you can use it again.)

Roast the Onions

Preheat the oven to 375°F (190°C). Turn on the convection fan if you have one.

Position the onions in a small baking pan with their root end down. Roast until tender all the way through, 60 to 90 minutes. Remove from the oven and rest until cool enough to handle and you're ready to serve. Trim away the root end and remove the skin. Season with salt and pepper. Serve whole or cut in half.

Grill the Garlic Scapes

Build and tend an aromatic fire in your firepit, burning down to a thick bed of glowing hot coals. Alternatively, fire up your barbecue or grill.

Bring a large pot of water to a boil. Carefully drop in the garlic scapes and blanch just until they turn bright green and tenderize, 1 minute or so. Drain the scapes. Grill the scapes, turning frequently, until tender and lightly charred, 5 minutes or so. Reserve.

recipe continues

Serves 4 as a vegetable main or 6 as a side

Crispy Shallots

4 cups (1 L) vegetable oil, for frying

4 shallots, thinly sliced crosswise and separated into rings

½ cup (125 mL) cornstarch

½ teaspoon (2 mL) sea salt

Freshly ground pepper

Whole Roasted Onions, Grilled Garlic Scapes, and Chive Flowers

4 large white or yellow onions, unpeeled, root end trimmed

Sea salt

Freshly ground pepper

4 garlic scapes

A handful of fresh chive flowers, torn into small pieces (or a handful of fresh chives, thinly sliced)

Nutmeg Soubise

4 tablespoons (60 mL) butter

1 pound (450 g) yellow onions, halved and thinly sliced

½ teaspoon (2 mL) sea salt

¼ cup (60 mL) all-purpose flour

½ teaspoon (2 mL) ground nutmeg

1 cup (250 mL) whole milk

1 cup (250 mL) heavy (35%) cream

1 teaspoon (5 mL) sherry vinegar

Make the Nutmeg Soubise

Toss the butter into a saucepan over medium-high heat. Swirl gently as it melts, steams, foams, and eventually lightly browns. Stir in the onions and salt, reduce the heat to low, cover tightly, and slowly, patiently cook, stirring frequently, until deliciously caramelized, 20 minutes or so. Stir in the flour and nutmeg. Transfer to a high-speed blender or food processor, add the milk, cream, and sherry vinegar, and purée until smooth. Return the sauce to the pot over medium heat and cook, stirring constantly, until slowly simmering and thickened, 5 minutes or so. Remove from the heat.

Assemble the Dish

Pour a puddle of the nutmeg soubise onto plates. Nestle a whole baked onion on top. Top with a grilled garlic scape and crispy shallots. Sprinkle with chive flowers.

many peas and mint salad

minted pea purée

We grow many types of peas on our farm and harvest them at various times in their life cycle. We love their sweet shoots and aromatic flowers as much as their tender fresh seeds, the peas, and their often edible pods. We also nurture a dozen or so different types of mint. For a few glorious weeks each summer, while all these flavours are at their peak, we toss them all together in this simple and refreshing salad.

When puréed, some mint varieties lose their bright colour. For bright green purée, choose a mint with bright green leaves, avoiding darker plants.

Make the Minted Pea Purée

Heat the canola oil in a small saucepan over medium heat. Add the shallots and garlic and cook, stirring frequently, until soft and fragrant but not browned, 2 or 3 minutes. Add the water and bring to a simmer. Add the peas, season with salt and pepper, and cook until bright green and tender, just a minute or two. Transfer the works to a high-speed blender and carefully purée until smooth. (Hot liquids are dangerous—they can violently erupt. For safety, drape a kitchen towel over the blender, start slowly, then gradually increase the speed.) Add the mint and purée until smooth. Reserve or transfer to a resealable container and refrigerate for up to 3 days.

Toss Together the Pea and Mint Salad

Combine the peas, pea shoots and flowers, mint leaves, and pickled red onions. Lightly toss with pickling juices until evenly dressed. Spoon the minted pea purée onto plates. Top with a tangle of salad and garnish with the reserved mint sprigs.

Serves 4 as a vegetable main or 8 as a side

Minted Pea Purée

2 tablespoons (30 mL) extra-virgin canola or olive oil

2 shallots, minced

2 garlic cloves, minced

½ cup (125 mL) water

8 ounces (225 g) fresh peas, shucked

½ teaspoon (2 mL) sea salt

Freshly ground pepper

1 cup (250 mL) fresh mint leaves

Pea and Mint Salad

1 pound (450 g) various types of fresh peas (shucking peas, snap peas cut in half lengthwise, snow peas cut into slivers), pea shoots, and flowers

A few handfuls of fresh mint leaves and tender stems, from various varieties if possible, a few sprigs reserved for garnish

1 cup (250 mL) Pickled Red Onions and pickling juices (page 222)

mushy green beans and tarragon

carrot almond butter, crispy onions

Serves 6 to 8 as a vegetable side

Sometimes it's okay to overcook green vegetables, but there needs to be a good reason. Green beans are super tasty raw right out of the garden, as well as lightly steamed or barely cooked, but they also have a special savouriness that emerges when they soften, long after they've lost their fresh flavour and colour. Here they're served with a memorable condiment from a few rows over in the garden: earthy carrots, roasted until deliciously caramelized, simmered tender in fresh carrot juice, and smoothly puréed with almond butter.

Make the Carrot Almond Butter

Preheat the oven to 350°F (180°C). Turn on the convection fan if you have one.

Using a juicer, juice about half the carrots until you have 1 cup (250 mL) of juice. Chop the remaining carrots. In a small roasting pan, toss the carrots with the vegetable oil and salt. Roast, stirring occasionally, until browned and lightly crisped, 45 minutes or so. Transfer to a small saucepan, add the carrot juice, and bring to a low boil over medium heat. Cover, reduce the heat to a simmer, and cook, stirring occasionally, until the carrots are soft, 15 minutes or so. Without uncovering, remove from the heat and let sit for 15 minutes. Transfer to a food processor and add the almond butter, miso, hot sauce, and apple cider vinegar. Purée until smooth. Reserve or transfer to a resealable container and refrigerate for up to 3 days.

Fry the Crispy Onions

Heat the vegetable oil in a large pot or deep-fryer over medium-high heat until it reaches 375°F (190°C) on a deep-fat thermometer. In a small bowl, toss together the onions, cornstarch, and salt. Carefully transfer the onions to the hot oil and fry, stirring constantly with a skimmer or slotted spoon, until golden brown and crispy, just 1 to 2 minutes. Adjust the heat to maintain the ideal frying temperature of 365°F (185°C). Drain on paper towel. Lightly season with salt and pepper. (Cool, strain, and refrigerate the frying oil so you can use it again.)

Make the Mushy Green Beans

Heat a large, heavy skillet over high heat. Add the vegetable oil and beans and season with salt and pepper. Sauté briefly to combine, then cover tightly and cook, without shaking the pan, until browned on one side, 5 minutes or so. Adjust the heat to the lowest setting. Add the water, cover tightly, and braise, shaking the skillet occasionally, until the beans are tender and the water has mostly evaporated, 10 minutes or so. Toss with tarragon. Serve with spoonfuls of carrot almond butter. Sprinkle with crispy onions.

Carrot Almond Butter

2 pounds (900 g) orange carrots, peeled, divided

1 tablespoon (15 mL) vegetable oil

1 teaspoon (5 mL) sea salt

½ cup (125 mL) almond butter

1 tablespoon (15 mL) yellow miso

1 teaspoon (5 mL) of your favourite hot sauce

1 teaspoon (5 mL) apple cider vinegar

Crispy Onions

4 cups (1 L) vegetable oil, for frying

1 large white onion, thinly sliced and separated into rings

½ cup (125 mL) cornstarch

½ teaspoon (2 mL) sea salt

Mushy Green Beans

1 tablespoon (15 mL) vegetable oil

1 pound (450 g) green beans, trimmed

½ teaspoon (2 mL) sea salt

Freshly ground pepper

1 cup (250 mL) water

Leaves from a handful of fresh tarragon sprigs

greens, herbs, and flowers
farmhouse dressing

You can taste the essence of a garden in its salad, the season's sun in a bowl. We extravagantly share our farm's best, with as many ingredients as we can, and try to craft a salad so every bite is different. The secrets are simple. We've learned how to toss together the very best greens and tender vegetables we can possibly grow with handfuls of fresh, aromatic herb leaves and a sharp dressing.

Make the Farmhouse Dressing

Measure the ingredients into a 2-cup (500 mL) mason jar. Screw on the lid and shake vigorously until thoroughly mixed and smoothly combined. Store in the refrigerator for up to 1 month. Give it another brief shake before using.

Toss Together the Salad

Gently and thoroughly toss together the greens and herbs in a large festive bowl. Add half or more of the farmhouse dressing and toss well. Serve communally in the bowl or on individual plates. Sprinkle with lots of flower confetti.

Farmhouse Dressing (makes extra)

½ cup (125 mL) extra-virgin canola or olive oil

½ cup (125 mL) apple cider vinegar

¼ cup (60 mL) pure liquid honey or pure maple syrup

1 tablespoon (15 mL) of your favourite mustard

1 teaspoon (5 mL) sea salt

Greens and Herbs

Handfuls of various lettuces, greens, baby greens and tender leaves

Lots of fresh herb leaves (basil, parsley, mint, dill, fennel, cilantro, anise hyssop, and lemon verbena are favourites)

Flower Confetti

Handfuls of fresh herb, vegetable, and other edible flowers, whole or torn or shredded into petals, smaller pieces, or slivers (nasturtiums, marigolds, viola, bachelor's button, borage, arugula, mustard, sage, fennel, dill, chive, and cilantro are favourites)

confit tomato, poblano, and garlic

Classically, to confit means to slowly cook and then cool meat in its own rendered fat as a means of preservation and a path to deep flavour. You can pay homage to the method in the farmhouse vegetable kitchen when tomatoes are at their seasonal peak, with a fragrant oil instead of animal fat. For best results choose fleshier tomato varietals—the juicier ones are best enjoyed raw—and take the time to blanch to remove the skin first. Serve as a side dish, with any rice or grain as a vegetable main dish, tossed with your favourite freshly cooked pasta, lightly mashed as a bruschetta topping or sauce for any meat or fish, or refrigerate and enjoy in a delectable salad tomorrow.

Prepare the Tomatoes

Half fill a large bowl with ice water. Bring a large pot of water to a full furious boil over high heat, then reduce to a slow, steady simmer. Carefully drop the tomatoes, one at a time, into the boiling water and stir gently with a skimmer or slotted spoon just long enough to loosen the skin, 20 seconds or so. Lift the tomatoes from the boiling water and plunge them into the ice water so they don't overcook. Remove from water and rest until cool. With the tip of a small knife, peel back the skin and discard.

Slowly Confit the Tomatoes, Garlic, and Chilies

Preheat the oven to 250°F (120°C). Turn on the convection fan if you have one.

Season the tomatoes with salt and nestle them into a 13 x 9-inch (3.5 L) baking dish with the poblanos, garlic, and herb sprigs. Sprinkle evenly with the bay leaves, fennel seeds, coriander seeds, and cumin seeds. Pour in the canola oil. Cover the pan with foil and tightly seal. Bake until fragrant and tender, 3 hours or so. Remove from the oven and rest, covered, 1 hour longer. Use immediately or transfer to a resealable container and refrigerate for up to 5 days.

Serves 4 as a vegetable main or 8 as a side

12 ripe plum tomatoes or similar varietal with more flesh than juice, bottoms lightly scored crosswise

1 teaspoon (5 mL) sea salt

2 or 3 poblano peppers or similar fresh medium-heat varietal, halved, stems and seeds removed, thinly sliced crosswise

Cloves from 2 heads of garlic, peeled and woody ends trimmed

2 or 3 fresh herb sprigs (rosemary, thyme, savory, sage, or oregano)

4 bay leaves, broken into small pieces

1 tablespoon (15 mL) fennel seeds

1 tablespoon (15 mL) coriander seeds

1 tablespoon (15 mL) cumin seeds

1 cup (250 mL) extra-virgin canola or olive oil

grilled zucchini

green coriander seed salsa

Serves 6 to 8 as a vegetable side

On the farm, every season the same things always seem to happen at the same time, micro seasons that you come to anticipate and appreciate. Each year there's an intense time when long-awaited tomatoes, tender summer squashes, and various fragrant garden herbs are all at their peak. They taste so good together, we're lucky they grow together, and no wonder they're found together throughout the world of cuisine.

Make the Green Coriander Seed Salsa

In a large bowl, whisk together the canola oil, lime zest and juice, honey, jalapeño, and salt. Add the tomatoes, cucumber, green onions, and cilantro. Lightly and thoroughly toss together. Taste and adjust seasoning. Reserve at room temperature for an hour or two or transfer to a resealable container and refrigerate for up to 3 days.

Grill the Zucchini

Build and tend an aromatic fire in your firepit, burning down to a thick bed of glowing hot coals. Alternatively, fire up your barbecue or grill.

Lightly rub the zucchini with the vegetable oil and salt. Grill, turning frequently, until tender and lightly charred, 10 minutes or so. Serve with the green coriander seed salsa.

Green Coriander Seed Salsa

2 tablespoons (30 mL) extra-virgin canola or olive oil

Zest and juice of 2 limes (or 1 lemon)

1 tablespoon (15 mL) pure liquid honey

A fresh jalapeño pepper or two, stem and seeds removed, finely minced

1 teaspoon (5 mL) sea salt

1 pound (450 g) various varieties of sun-ripe tomatoes, halved, quartered, or cut into small bite-size pieces

1 garden or English cucumber, peeled, seeded, and diced

2 or 3 green onions, trimmed and thinly sliced crosswise

1 or 2 flowering cilantro plants (separate to yield 1 cup/250 mL minced leaves and tender stems and as much as 1 cup/250 mL green coriander seeds)

Grilled Zucchini

2 pounds (900 g) zucchini or other tender green or yellow summer squash, trimmed and halved lengthwise

2 tablespoons (30 mL) vegetable oil

Sea salt

grilled summer squash
grilled corn poblano relish

We grow many types of summer squashes, tender varieties that we harvest and enjoy long before their skins and seeds harden. Their sweet flavour tends to be much subtler than that of their stronger winter cousins, but they're also much easier to cook. Their tender flesh is particularly good grilled, as it chars easily and cooks quickly. While your grill is fired up you can also craft a delicious condiment that balances bright spiciness with charred corn and medium-heat poblano peppers.

Make the Grilled Corn Poblano Relish
Build and tend an aromatic fire in your firepit, burning down to a thick bed of glowing hot coals. Alternatively, fire up your barbecue or grill.

Position the garlic heads to one side and bake until bubbling juices ooze from the tops, 20 minutes or so. Place the lemon halves face down on the grill and cook until softened and lightly charred. Lightly rub the poblanos, corn, and onion slices with vegetable oil and season with salt. Grill, turning occasionally, until the vegetables are tender and lightly charred, 10 minutes or so. Remove and reserve.

Transfer the poblanos and red onions to a food processor. Use a serrated knife to slice off the tops of the garlic heads. Carefully squeeze the oozing garlic cloves into the food processor. Squeeze in the lemon pulp and juice, discarding the seeds. Pulse the mixture until coarsely chopped and thoroughly mixed. Shave the kernels from the cobs into a small bowl. Add the poblano mixture and oregano and stir to combine. Use immediately or transfer to a resealable container and refrigerate for up to 5 days.

Grill the Summer Squash
Lightly rub the squash with vegetable oil, salt, and pepper. Grill, turning occasionally, until tender and lightly charred, 15 minutes or so. Serve with the grilled corn poblano relish.

Serves 6 to 8 as a vegetable side

Grilled Corn Poblano Relish

2 heads of garlic

1 lemon, halved crosswise

2 poblano peppers, halved, stems and seeds removed

2 ears of fresh corn, shucked

2 red onions, cut into 4 thick slices, rings kept intact

Vegetable oil, for grilling

Sea salt

Leaves and tender stems from 3 or 4 sprigs of fresh oregano, minced

Grilled Summer Squash

2 pounds (900 g) summer squash, yellow squash, or zucchini, trimmed and halved lengthwise

Vegetable oil, for grilling

Sea salt

Freshly ground pepper

basil ratatouille and swiss chard wraps

tomato marigold salsa

The peak freshness of our own farmed vegetables inspires us to consider their individual culinary needs as we craft one of the world's great vegetable dishes. Classic ratatouille slowly builds layers of flavour, enhancing each new vegetable without damaging the last. You can enjoy it on its own as a delicious side dish or elevate it even further into a Swiss chard wrap. Marigolds and tomatoes grow together on our organic farm, the fragrant flowers serving as a deterrent to various pests. But marigold isn't just a pretty flower; its delicate herb-like flavours go well with sunny-ripe tomatoes. Its unique citrus-like fragrance is even stronger in its leaves, making it one of our favourite herbs.

Makes 8 basil ratatouille vegetable side dishes or 8 to 12 swiss chard wraps

Tomato Marigold Salsa

2 or 3 ripe plum tomatoes or similar varietal with more flesh than juice, quartered

1 jalapeño or serrano pepper or other high-heat varietal, stem and seeds removed

¼ cup (60 mL) Pickled Red Onions and pickling juices (page 222)

½ teaspoon (2 mL) sea salt

24 marigold leaves, lightly chopped, a few reserved for garnish

24 marigold flowers, a few reserved for garnish

Basil Ratatouille

1 large Italian eggplant, unpeeled, trimmed and cut into 1-inch (2.5 cm) cubes

1 teaspoon (5 mL) sea salt

6 tablespoons (90 mL) extra-virgin olive oil, divided

2 yellow onions, cut into medium dice

Cloves from 1 head of garlic, thinly sliced

½ teaspoon (2 mL) Red Chili Flakes (page 219) or store-bought

2 red bell peppers, halved, stems and seeds removed, finely diced

1 zucchini, trimmed, quartered lengthwise, and cut into bite-size cubes

1 yellow squash, trimmed, quartered lengthwise, and cut into bite-size cubes

3 to 4 large ripe tomatoes (about 1 pound/450 g), cut into bite-size cubes

1 bunch of fresh basil, 2 sprigs reserved, remaining leaves tightly rolled and thinly sliced

Swiss Chard Wraps

8 to 12 Swiss chard leaves, centre stalks removed

Make the Tomato Marigold Salsa

Combine the tomatoes, jalapeño, pickled red onions and their juices, and salt in a food processor and pulse until coarsely chopped and thoroughly mixed. Add the marigold leaves and flowers and pulse briefly to combine. Reserve or transfer to a resealable container and refrigerate for up to 3 days.

Make the Basil Ratatouille

In a small bowl, thoroughly toss together the eggplant and salt. Transfer to a colander or strainer and drain for 30 minutes to an hour. Transfer to few layered paper towels and blot dry. Heat 4 tablespoons (60 mL) of the olive oil in a large, heavy skillet or non-stick pan over high heat and fry the eggplant, turning occasionally, until deliciously golden brown, 10 minutes or so. Remove the eggplant and reserve.

recipe continues

Add the remaining 2 tablespoons (30 mL) olive oil and the onions to the pan and slowly, patiently cook, stirring frequently, until golden brown, 10 minutes or so. Reduce the heat to medium, stir in the garlic and chili flakes, and cook just until fragrant, a minute or so. Stir in the bell peppers. Cook until the textures soften, colours brighten, and flavours emerge, 2 minutes or so. Stir in the zucchini and squash and cook just long enough to awaken as well, 2 minutes more. Gently stir in the tomatoes and the reserved basil sprigs. Cover and cook at a slow, steady simmer, without stirring but occasionally gently shaking the pan, just until the tomatoes fully release their moisture, 10 minutes or so. Taste and adjust seasoning. Remove the wilted basil sprigs and discard. Gently stir in the eggplant and sliced basil. Remove from the heat. Use for the Swiss chard wraps, or transfer to a resealable container and refrigerate for up to 3 days.

Make the Swiss Chard Wraps

Bring a pot of salted water to a slow, steady simmer. Briefly dip each chard leaf in the hot water, stirring gently just long enough to wilt. Drain and lay flat on paper towel.

Neatly line a 2-inch (5 cm) tall and 3 or 4-inch (8 to 10 cm) wide ring mould or standard ramekin with a leaf or two, allowing the ends to hang over the edges. Fill the mould with the ratatouille, pressing firmly with the back of a spatula to level the stew with the rim of the mould. Fold the leaf ends over the ratatouille, pressing firmly to create a tidy wrapped package. Invert then carefully remove the mould and transfer to a serving platter or individual plates. Serve with the tomato marigold salsa.

lion's mane mushroom steaks
brown butter béarnaise sauce

Serves 6 to 8 as a vegetable side

The dense texture, sweet, earthy flavour, and sheer size of lion's mane mushrooms give them the strength and flavour of a steak. They're one of the varieties that emerge from inoculated maple logs on our mushroom farm in the back woods. Classic béarnaise sauce accents rich hollandaise with bright, tangy tarragon and sharp vinegar.

Brown the Butter
Toss the butter into a small saucepan over medium-high heat. Swirl gently as it melts, steams, foams, and eventually lightly browns. Pour into a small bowl and rest at room temperature until cool, at least an hour, even overnight. Do not refrigerate.

Make the Brown Butter Béarnaise Sauce
Combine the white wine, white wine vinegar, shallot, and peppercorns in a small saucepan. Simmer over medium heat until the liquid is reduced to a syrup and has nearly disappeared. Remove from the heat.

Bring a medium saucepan with 2 inches (5 cm) of water to a bare simmer over low heat. In a heat-resistant medium bowl, whisk together the egg yolks and water until frothy. Position the bowl over the simmering water and continue whisking until the egg mixture gradually heats and thickens, 3 minutes or so. Remove the pot and bowl from the heat. Continue whisking while slowly drizzling in every drop of the brown butter (including the sediment). Whisk until smooth. Whisk in the shallot mixture and minced tarragon. Serve immediately or tightly cover the bowl with plastic wrap and reposition the bowl over the warm water (off the heat). Rest for no more than 20 minutes or so.

recipe continues

Brown Butter Béarnaise Sauce
¾ cup (175 mL) butter

¼ cup (60 mL) dry white wine

¼ cup (60 mL) white wine vinegar or sherry vinegar

1 shallot, finely minced

12 black peppercorns, cracked

3 large egg yolks

1½ teaspoons (7 mL) water

6 sprigs of fresh tarragon, leaves from 4 minced, 2 reserved for garnish

Lion's Mane Mushroom Steaks
2 pounds (900 g) lion's mane mushrooms, cut into 1 to 2-inch-thick (2.5 to 5 cm) slices

2 tablespoons (30 mL) vegetable oil, for grilling, or ¼ cup (60 mL) butter or vegetable oil, for pan-frying

Sea salt

Freshly ground pepper

Grill the Lion's Mane Mushrooms

Build and tend an aromatic fire in your firepit, burning down to a thick bed of glowing hot coals. Alternatively, fire up your barbecue or grill.

Lightly rub the mushroom steaks with vegetable oil and season with salt and pepper. Grill, turning occasionally, until tender and lightly browned, 15 minutes or so. Serve with brown butter béarnaise sauce, garnish with the reserved tarragon sprigs.

or

Pan-Fry the Lion's Mane Mushrooms

Lightly season the mushroom steaks with salt and pepper. Melt the butter in a large, heavy skillet or non-stick skillet over medium-high heat. Position the mushroom steaks in the sizzling butter, swirling gently to evenly distribute. Pan-fry, adjusting the heat to maintain a flavourful sizzle without burning, and flipping occasionally, until golden brown and crispy, 15 minutes or so. Serve with brown butter béarnaise sauce, garnish with the reserved tarragon sprigs.

grilled eggplant baba ganoush

za'atar-spiced eggplant chips

Baba ganoush comes from the tasty traditions of Lebanese and Middle Eastern cooking. It's one of the world's great dips, perfect for sharing, and an incredible transformation of a spongy, weirdly chewy, and bitter raw vegetable. Cooked properly, eggplant becomes a marvel of smooth, luscious texture. To unlock that potential, you can roast the vegetable whole or, for even more flavour, get grilling. At the other end of the texture spectrum, bake eggplant slices into crisp dippers for the dip dipping ahead!

Grill the Eggplant and Make the Baba Ganoush

Build and tend an aromatic fire in your firepit, burning down to a thick bed of glowing hot coals. Alternatively, fire up your barbecue or grill.

Lightly rub the eggplant's cut side with vegetable oil and season with salt. Grill flesh side down, turning and repositioning occasionally, flipping once or twice, until softened and lightly charred, 20 minutes or so. Remove and rest until cool.

Transfer the eggplants with their charred skin to a food processor. Add the tahini, yogurt, lemon zest and juice, garlic, cumin, and chili flakes. Purée until smooth. Taste and adjust the salt and lemon as needed. Reserve or transfer to a resealable container and refrigerate for up to 3 days. Garnish with basil just before serving.

Bake the Za'atar-Spiced Eggplant Chips

Preheat the oven to 250°F (120°C). Turn on the convection fan if you have one. Line 2 baking sheets with silicone baking mats or parchment paper.

Brush both sides of the eggplant with olive oil and tightly arrange the eggplant slices on the baking sheets. Season lightly with salt, and generously sprinkle with sesame za'atar. Bake until dry and lightly browned, exactly 75 minutes. Remove and rest until cool and crisp.

Serve the grilled eggplant baba ganoush with lots of za'atar-spiced eggplant chips for dipping.

Makes 6 cups (1.5 L) baba ganoush, enough for 6 to 8 to share as a vegetable side

Grilled Eggplant Baba Ganoush

4 large globe or Italian eggplants (about 4 pounds/ 1.8 kg), halved lengthwise

¼ cup (60 mL) vegetable oil

Sea salt

½ cup (125 mL) tahini

½ cup (125 mL) natural plain full-fat yogurt or plain Greek yogurt

Zest and juice of 1 lemon

2 garlic cloves, finely grated with a microplane or finely minced

1 teaspoon (5 mL) ground cumin

1 teaspoon (5 mL) Red Chili Flakes (page 219) or store-bought

Fresh basil leaves, thinly sliced, for garnish

Za'atar-Spiced Eggplant Chips

4 Japanese or 1 large Italian eggplant (about 1 pound/ 450 g), sliced crosswise into very thin rounds

½ cup (125 mL) olive oil or vegetable oil

½ teaspoon (2 mL) sea salt

2 tablespoons (30 mL) Sesame Za'atar (page 220)

fennel marmalade

This all-purpose condiment brightens any vegetarian, fish, or meat dish. The distinctive anise flavour of the vegetable deepens through slow cooking and is then enlivened with lemon, anise liqueur, and just enough spicy heat. As fennel grows it produces deliciously fragrant flowers and intensely aromatic seeds. Green fennel seeds, harvested before they toughen and dry, are the perfect finishing touch.

Heat the olive oil in a medium saucepan over medium heat. Add the dried fennel seeds and stir until sizzling and fragrant, just a minute or so. Stir in the sliced fennel, onion, and garlic. Cover, reduce the heat to low, and slowly cook, stirring frequently to prevent browning, until the fennel is softened and reduced, 45 minutes or so. Stir in the anise liqueur, lemon zest and juice, salt, and chili flakes. Cover and cook for 15 minutes more. Remove from the heat. Stir in the fennel flowers and green fennel seeds. Use immediately or transfer to a resealable container and refrigerate for up to 1 week.

2 tablespoons (30 mL) olive oil

2 tablespoons (30 mL) dried fennel seeds

2 fennel bulbs, trimmed, halved, cored, and thinly sliced

1 yellow onion, thinly sliced

4 garlic cloves, minced

½ cup (125 mL) anise liqueur (Pernod, pastis, ouzo, anisette, Sambuca)

Zest and juice of 1 lemon

½ teaspoon (2 mL) sea salt

½ teaspoon (2 mL) Red Chili Flakes (page 219) or store-bought

A handful of fresh fennel flowers, lightly minced

2 tablespoons (30 mL) fresh green fennel seeds

fennel mustard pickle slaw

Mustard pickles are part of Atlantic Canada's culinary heritage and a frequent condiment at the inn. Our favourite recipe comes to us from legendary Nova Scotia chef Craig Flinn, an alumnus of our kitchen. We like to toss it with thinly shaved fennel bulb from our farm to create a delicious slaw that can be enjoyed as a bright condiment or a side dish of its own.

Slice the fennel bulbs lengthwise as thinly as possible. For very best results, use a mandoline. Toss together in a medium bowl with the reserved fennel fronds and mustard pickles. Serve immediately, or deepen the flavour by resting for an hour or two, or transfer to a resealable container and refrigerate for up to 5 days.

Serves 6 to 8 as a vegetable side

2 fennel bulbs, trimmed, halved, and cored, feathery fronds lightly chopped

2 cups (500 mL) Maritime Mustard Pickles (page 218)

fresh ice plant salsa

Ice plant is a slightly salty succulent and one of the most unusual plants on our farm. It's a beach plant that tolerates salt water by holding it in tiny hairs on its leaves that reflect light like sparkly ice crystals. It's also highly invasive, so we grow it in enclosed beds to limit its spread. Ice plant is excellent raw and strong enough to be grilled. Its crisp texture and sweet-savoury flavour are highlighted in this simple fresh salsa. Enjoy as a dip, topping, or all-purpose condiment.

Toss all the ingredients together in a medium bowl. Serve immediately, garnished with reserved ice plant sprigs, or transfer to a resealable container and refrigerate for up to 3 days.

Makes about 4 cups (1 L), enough for 6 to 8 to share as a vegetable side

2 large sunny-ripe tomatoes, finely diced

A handful of ice plant leaves and tender stems (see page 229), finely chopped, a few sprigs reserved for garnish

8 green onions, thinly sliced

1 poblano pepper, stem and seeds removed, finely minced

Zest and juice of 2 limes

½ teaspoon (2 mL) sea salt

cauliflower chickpea fritters

broccoli garlic sauce

Simple techniques elevate broccoli and cauliflower in this delicious side dish. Smooth white cauliflower purée and chickpea flour make gluten- and dairy-free yet memorably crisp fritters. Briefly cooked broccoli is smoothly puréed into a bright green sauce with lots of mellowed garlic.

Make the Broccoli Garlic Sauce

In a medium saucepan, cook the butter and onion over medium heat, stirring frequently, until the onion is fragrant and softened but not browned, 3 to 4 minutes. Stir in the garlic, reduce the heat, and continue cooking, stirring frequently, just until the garlic is fragrant and softened but not browned, 2 or 3 minutes more. Add the water and salt and increase the heat to a boil. Add the broccoli, reduce the heat to a simmer, cover, and cook until bright green and tender, 7 to 8 minutes.

Transfer to a high-speed blender and carefully purée until smooth. (Hot liquids are dangerous—they can violently erupt. For safety, drape a kitchen towel over the blender, start slowly, then gradually increase the speed.) Use immediately or transfer to a resealable container and refrigerate for up to 3 days. Gently reheat before serving.

Make the Fritter Batter

In a medium saucepan, combine the cauliflower stems, 1 cup (250 mL) florets, and the water. Bring to a simmer over medium heat, then cover and cook until the vegetables are mushy, 10 minutes or so. Transfer to a food processor and purée until smooth. Add the chickpea flour, curry powder, cumin seeds, fennel seeds, chili flakes, salt, and baking soda. Process until thoroughly mixed. Transfer to a medium bowl. Stir in the remaining cauliflower florets, thoroughly coating them in batter. Use immediately or transfer to a resealable container and refrigerate for up to 3 days.

Fry the Cauliflower Chickpea Fritters

Heat the vegetable oil in a large pot or deep-fryer over medium-high heat until it reaches 375°F (190°C) on a deep-fat thermometer. Using 2 spoons, the first to scoop, the second to release the batter, gently drop spoonfuls of the batter into the hot oil. Work in batches so you don't crowd the pot. Adjust the heat to maintain the ideal frying temperature of 365°F (185°C). Fry, stirring gently with a skimmer or slotted spoon, until golden brown and crispy, 2 to 3 minutes. Drain briefly on paper towel. Lightly season with salt. (Carefully cool, strain, and refrigerate the frying oil so you can use it again.)

Serve the fritters with the broccoli garlic sauce, garnished with broccoli flowers.

Makes 24 or so fritters, enough for 4 to 6 as a vegetable side

Broccoli Garlic Sauce

4 tablespoons (60 mL) butter (or 2 tablespoons/30 mL vegetable oil)

1 large yellow onion, finely diced

Cloves from 1 head of garlic, thinly sliced

1 cup (250 mL) water

1 teaspoon (5 mL) sea salt

1 bunch of broccoli, cut into florets, tender stems finely diced

Cauliflower Chickpea Fritters

1 head of cauliflower, broken into small florets, tender inner stem chopped

1½ cups (375 mL) water

2 cups (500 mL) chickpea flour

2 tablespoons (30 mL) curry powder

1 tablespoon (15 mL) cumin seeds

1 tablespoon (15 mL) fennel seeds

1 tablespoon (15 mL) Red Chili Flakes (page 219) or store-bought

1 teaspoon (5 mL) sea salt

½ teaspoon (2 mL) baking soda

4 cups (1 L) vegetable oil, for frying

A handful of broccoli flowers from a past-harvest plant, for garnish

grilled broccolini
oyster garlic glaze

Serves 6 to 8 as a vegetable side

Broccolini is one of many brassicas that we grow on our farm. It's not baby broccoli but a separate variety with thinner stems, hearty florets, and a texture perfect for grilling because, unlike broccoli, the deliciously sweet florets don't overcook before the stalks are done. Like other bitter hearty greens, broccolini benefits from the big, bold finishing flavours of expertly browned garlic and savoury oyster sauce simmered into a last-second glaze.

4 bunches of broccolini or gai lan (about 2 pounds/900 g total)

2 tablespoons (30 mL) vegetable oil

2 garlic cloves, finely minced

3 tablespoons (45 mL) oyster sauce

Grill the Broccolini
Build and tend an aromatic fire in your firepit, burning down to a thick bed of glowing hot coals. Alternatively, fire up your barbecue or grill.

Grill the broccolini, turning frequently, until bright green, tender, and lightly charred, 5 minutes or so.

Glaze the Broccolini
Heat the vegetable oil in a large non-stick or heavy-duty skillet over medium-high heat. Add the garlic and sauté until lightly browned and fragrant. Remove from the heat. Working quickly, add the oyster sauce and grilled broccolini. Swirl and toss until the broccolini is evenly coated with the garlicky sauce.

roasted brussels sprouts, bean sprouts, broccoli sprouts, and cashews

kimchi miso dressing

Every plant on our farm first emerges from its seed and pokes through the soil as a single cotyledon sprout. Some seeds, like broccoli, we start in our sprout house (see page 20) for those first tentative sprouts; some beans and legumes we coax into larger but still tender sprouts; and some plants, like Brussels sprouts, produce further tender sprouts of their own as they mature. All these sprouts are delicious served together and dressed with an easy savoury dressing from the global pantry for a richly satisfying side dish.

Make the Kimchi Miso Dressing
Measure the kimchi and juices, vegetable oil, miso, rice vinegar, and mustard into a small food processor. Purée until smooth. Reserve or transfer to a resealable container and refrigerate for up to 5 days.

Roast the Brussels Sprouts
Preheat the oven to 425°F (220°C). Turn on the convection fan if you have one.

Toss together the Brussels sprouts and vegetable oil in a large cast-iron pan, ovenproof skillet, or large roasting pan. Lightly season with salt and pepper. Roast until tender and charred, occasionally shaking and settling the pan, 20 minutes or so. Remove from the oven. Immediately stir in the kimchi miso dressing and mung bean sprouts, allowing the residual heat to wilt the tender sprouts. Serve sprinkled with cashews and broccoli sprouts.

Serves 6 to 8 as a vegetable side

Kimchi Miso Dressing
½ cup (125 mL) prepared kimchi and juices

¼ cup (60 mL) vegetable oil

¼ cup (60 mL) yellow miso

2 tablespoons (30 mL) rice vinegar or cider vinegar

1 teaspoon (5 mL) yellow mustard

Roasted Brussels Sprouts
2 pounds (900 g) Brussels sprouts, trimmed

2 tablespoons (30 mL) vegetable oil or reserved animal fat (see page 3)

Sea salt

Freshly ground pepper

1 package (about 12 ounces/340 g) fresh mung bean sprouts

1 cup (250 mL) unsalted roasted cashews

A handful or two of broccoli sprouts or other savoury, snappy fresh microgreens (kale, radish, turnip, or cress)

whole roasted cauliflower

ancho cider poached, spiced brown butter hollandaise

This delicious showstopper elevates cauliflower to its rightful status as a main course. The secret to a roasted whole cauliflower, tender inside yet crispy and browned on the outside, is to poach it first. As it poaches, the spices and oil settle into the nooks and crannies of the cauliflower, where they later help it caramelize in the dry heat of the oven. To honour the humble vegetable, richly sauce it with a classic hollandaise deepened with patiently browned butter and enlivened with mysterious spices.

Poach the Cauliflower

In a large pot, combine the apple cider, apple cider vinegar, vegetable oil, salt, chilies, fennel seeds, and bay leaves. Bring to a full simmer over medium-high heat. Add the cauliflower heads, nestling them sideways in the pot. Reduce the heat to a bare simmer, cover, and poach, turning occasionally, until evenly cooked through and tender, 20 minutes or so. Carefully transfer to a baking sheet or roasting pan.

Roast the Cauliflower

Preheat the oven to 375°F (190°C). Turn on the convection fan if you have one.

Roast the whole cauliflowers until lightly and evenly browned, charred, and crispy, 45 minutes or so.

Brown the Butter

Toss the butter into a small saucepan over medium-high heat. Swirl gently as it melts, steams, foams, and eventually lightly browns. Remove from the heat and swirl in the cinnamon and cumin. Rest at room temperature until cool, at least an hour, even overnight. Do not refrigerate.

Make the Spiced Brown Butter Hollandaise

Bring a medium saucepan with 2 inches (5 cm) of water to a bare simmer over low heat. In a heat-resistant medium bowl, whisk together the egg yolks, water, and lemon zest and juice until frothy. Position the bowl over the simmering water and continue whisking until the egg mixture gradually heats and thickens, 3 minutes or so. Remove the pot and bowl from the heat. Continue whisking while slowly drizzling in every drop of the spiced brown butter (including the sediment). Whisk until smooth. Serve immediately with the roasted whole cauliflower, or tightly cover the bowl with plastic wrap and reposition the bowl over the warm water (off the heat). Rest for no more than 20 minutes or so.

Serves 4 as a vegetable main or 6 to 8 as a side

Whole Roasted Cauliflower

6 cups (1.5 L) fresh apple cider, apple juice, orange juice, or water

½ cup (125 mL) apple cider vinegar

½ cup (125 mL) vegetable oil

¼ cup (60 mL) sea salt

2 dried ancho chilies, stems and seeds removed, cracked into small pieces (or 2 tablespoons/30 mL ancho chili powder)

2 tablespoons (30 mL) fennel seeds

2 bay leaves

2 heads of cauliflower, leaves removed, ends of stems trimmed

Spiced Brown Butter Hollandaise

1 cup (250 mL) butter

½ teaspoon (2 mL) cinnamon

½ teaspoon (2 mL) ground cumin

4 large egg yolks

2 tablespoons (30 mL) water

Zest and juice of 1 lemon

cauliflower steaks

horseradish cauliflower cream

When you grow your own vegetables, you're inspired to use as much of the plant as possible. You can trim two thick steaks from the centre of a cauliflower head, roast them, and serve them with a delicious sauce crafted from . . . the rest of the cauliflower. Respecting the whole head this way is a graceful tribute to the hard work of whoever grew it.

Prep the Cauliflower
Cut each head of cauliflower in half through the stem, then trim off the rounded sides of each half to make four 2-inch-thick (5 cm) steaks. Chop the trimmed side pieces. Store in an resealable container and refrigerate for up to 3 days.

Make the Cauliflower Cream
In a small saucepan, combine the chopped cauliflower trimmings, white wine, and butter. Bring to a simmer over medium heat, cover, reduce the heat to low, and cook until very tender, 15 minutes or so. Transfer the works to a high-speed blender, add the horseradish, salt, and carefully purée until smooth. (Hot liquids are dangerous—they can violently erupt. For safety, drape a kitchen towel over the blender, start slowly, then gradually increase the speed.) Reserve or transfer to a resealable container and refrigerate for up to 3 days. Gently reheat before serving.

Pan-Roast the Cauliflower Steaks
Heat the vegetable oil in a large, heavy skillet over medium heat. Lightly season both sides of the steaks with salt and pepper. Working in batches if needed, evenly position the cauliflower steaks in the sizzling pan and slowly cook until the bottoms are evenly golden brown, 15 minutes or so. Using a metal spatula, carefully turn over and cook until golden brown on the bottom, 15 minutes or so more. If working in batches, keep the first batch warm in a 200°F (100°C) oven while you cook the remaining cauliflower steaks. Serve with spoonfuls of cauliflower cream and garnish with chives.

Serves 4 as a vegetable main or 6 to 8 as a side

Cauliflower Steaks

2 heads of cauliflower, leaves removed, ends of stems trimmed

¼ cup (60 mL) vegetable oil or reserved animal fat (see page 3)

Sea salt

Freshly ground pepper

Cauliflower Cream

Reserved cauliflower trimmings

2 cups (500 mL) dry white wine

4 tablespoons (60 mL) butter or extra-virgin canola or olive oil

¼ cup (60 mL) prepared horseradish

½ teaspoon (2 mL) sea salt

1 bunch of fresh chives, chopped, for garnish

wilted cabbage

tarragon, cream

Serves 4 to 6 as a vegetable side

Sometimes an ingredient or a cooking technique is so simple that we overlook how powerful it can be. Usually, cabbage is either the raw neutral base of coleslaw or cooked for so long that it nearly melts away. There's a flavour revelation in the middle, though, that we often miss—a simple middle step for this equally simple vegetable. The secret is meticulous knife work and high-heat searing. Take the time to cut the leaves as thinly as possible so they cook as quickly as possible. Cabbage cooked this way is sweet, juicy, and pleasingly tender without being soft. Rich cream and bright tarragon finish the transformation.

Heat a large, heavy pot or Dutch oven over highest heat. Add the oil, toss in the cabbage, season with salt and pepper, and cook, stirring continuously, searing, steaming, and softening until heated through and barely tender, stopping before the leaves begin releasing moisture, 5 minutes or so. Stir in the cream and tarragon leaves. Taste and adjust seasoning. Serve immediately, garnished with a few sprigs of tarragon.

2 tablespoons (30 mL) vegetable oil or reserved animal fat (see page 3)

1 white cabbage, quartered, cored, and very finely shredded

1 teaspoon (5 mL) sea salt

Freshly ground pepper

½ cup (125 mL) heavy (35%) cream

Leaves from 1 bunch of fresh tarragon, a few sprigs reserved for garnish

roasted butternut squash steaks

sage, pumpkin seed, and goat cheese pesto

Serves 4 as a vegetable side

The firm texture and nutty skin of butternut squash allow you to evenly cut it into thick steaks, which are easily roasted to maximize the vegetable's sweet flavour. A condiment of strong sage, crunchy pumpkin seeds, and rich goat cheese adds savoury balance.

Make the Sage, Pumpkin Seed, and Goat Cheese Pesto

In a food processor, combine the pumpkin seeds, sage, garlic, canola oil, salt, and chili flakes. Process into a smooth purée, scraping down the sides once or twice. Add the goat cheese and process until smooth. Reserve or transfer to a resealable container and refrigerate for up to 3 days.

Roast the Butternut Squash Steaks

Preheat the oven to 400°F (200°C). Turn on the convection fan if you have one.

Trim the ends from the squash, then cut crosswise into 4 thick rounds. Scrape out the seeds and stringy bits (2 rounds will be doughnut-shaped). Place the squash on a baking sheet or in a shallow baking pan. Evenly oil both sides of the squash rounds and lightly season with salt and pepper. Roast until golden brown and tender, 45 minutes or so. Top the roasted squash with sage, pumpkin seed, and goat cheese pesto.

Sage, Pumpkin Seed, and Goat Cheese Pesto

1 cup (250 mL) unsalted roasted pumpkin seeds

Leaves from 2 bunches of fresh sage (about 1 cup/250 mL)

4 garlic cloves, thinly sliced

¼ cup (60 mL) extra-virgin canola or olive oil

½ teaspoon (2 mL) sea salt

¼ teaspoon (1 mL) Red Chili Flakes (page 219) or store-bought

4 ounces (115 g) soft goat cheese

Roasted Butternut Squash Steaks

1 large butternut squash (2 pounds/900 g), unpeeled

2 tablespoons (30 mL) vegetable oil or reserved animal fat (see page 3)

Sea salt

Freshly ground pepper

maple-spiced sweet potato
cilantro cashew pesto

We grow many things well on our farm, but sweet potatoes are not one of them—our growing season is too short. So instead, we rely on farmers in much warmer climates to do it for us. Nonetheless they are a nutritional powerhouse, and one of my favourite vegetables. Baking is my preferred way to cook them. We do grow lots of fragrant cilantro, and through life-cycle harvesting we enjoy its aromatic leaves, green coriander seeds, and lacy white flowers. The pesto brings together lots of citrusy cilantro leaves and bright balancing flavours in a tasty condiment ready to complete a deliciously baked sweet potato.

Make the Cilantro Cashew Pesto

Measure the cilantro, cashews, garlic, canola oil, lemon zest and juice, cheese, and salt into a food processor. Purée until a smooth, bright paste emerges, scraping down the sides a few times along the way. Reserve or transfer to a resealable container and refrigerate for up to 5 days.

Make the Maple-Spiced Sweet Potato

Preheat the oven to 350°F (180°C). Turn on the convection fan if you have one. Line a baking sheet with a silicone baking mat or parchment paper.

Use the point of a small sharp knife to lightly score the surface of the sweet potatoes in a diamond pattern, making cuts ½ inch (1 cm) deep at ½-inch (1 cm) intervals. (For smaller side portions, no need to score the wedges.) Arrange the sweet potatoes cut side up on the prepared baking sheet and lightly oil the tops. Season with salt and pepper. Bake for 45 minutes. Carefully brush the potatoes with maple syrup and evenly sprinkle with the fennel seeds and coriander seeds. Continue baking until glazed and tender, 15 minutes or so more. Serve with a generous dollop of cilantro cashew pesto on top. Garnish with cilantro flowers, if any, and a few tender stems.

Cilantro Cashew Pesto

1 large bunch of fresh cilantro leaves and tender stems, any flowers and a few tender stems reserved for garnish

1 cup (250 mL) unsalted roasted cashews

4 garlic cloves, sliced

½ cup (125 mL) extra-virgin canola or olive oil

Zest and juice of 1 lemon

4 ounces (115 g) Parmigiano-Reggiano cheese, grated

½ teaspoon (2 mL) sea salt

Maple-Spiced Sweet Potato

2 large sweet potatoes, unpeeled, sliced in half lengthwise (cut each potato into 4 wedges for smaller side portions)

1 tablespoon (15 mL) vegetable oil, olive oil, or reserved animal fat (see page 3)

Sea salt

Freshly ground pepper

¼ cup (60 mL) pure maple syrup

1 tablespoon (15 mL) fennel seeds

1 tablespoon (15 mL) green coriander seeds

honey-roasted sunflower head

Rows of mesmerizing sunflowers dominate our Fire Garden every year. Their energetic flowers follow the sun throughout the day, forever turning their faces into the rays. All that effort eventually concentrates in their dry seeds to be snacked on by birds and humans. When those seeds are still young and tender, though, they have a delicious fresh green herbaceous flavour. After simply roasting them, just spoon out the tender seeds and enjoy as is or scatter over another vegetable dish.

Preheat the oven to 350°F (180°C). Turn on the convection fan if you have one. Line a baking sheet with a silicone baking mat or parchment paper.

In a small bowl, whisk together the honey, sunflower oil, salt, and pepper. Brush the honey mixture over the seed surface of the sunflowers. Position on the prepared baking sheet with as many flower petals as possible intact and roast until tender, 30 minutes or so, gently turning once at the 15-minute mark.

Serves 4 to 6 as a vegetable side

¼ cup (60 mL) pure liquid honey

¼ cup (60 mL) sunflower oil or olive oil

½ teaspoon (2 mL) sea salt

Freshly ground pepper

2 or 3 sunflower heads, picked when seed coatings are still soft, outer flower petals attached

vegetables and meat

cucumber radish salad with tarragon tonnato

radish sprouts

A classic creamy tonnato brightened with our farm's intensely fragrant tarragon stretches the flavour of cured fish into an umami-rich condiment for dressing vegetables. Our sprout house (see page 20) produces many microgreens like snappy, tangy radish sprouts. You can often find a variety of deliciously interchangeable microgreens at your local farmers' market.

Make the Tarragon Tonnato

Measure the tuna, anchovies, capers, garlic, lemon zest and juice, mustard, and hot sauce into a food processor. Purée into a smooth paste, scraping down the sides once or twice. Add the tarragon and pulse. Add the mayonnaise and purée until smooth. With the motor running, drizzle in the canola oil, forming a smooth, creamy emulsion. Use immediately or transfer to a resealable container and refrigerate for up to 3 days.

Make the Cucumber Radish Salad

In a large, festive serving bowl, toss together the cucumbers, radishes, and tarragon tonnato until evenly mixed and dressed. Serve topped with radish sprouts.

Serves 4 as a vegetable main or 6 to 8 as a side

Tarragon Tonnato (makes 2 cups/500 mL)

1 can (5 ounces/140 g) water-packed or oil-packed tuna, drained

1 can (2 ounces/50 g) oil-packed anchovy fillets, drained

1 tablespoon (15 mL) drained capers

2 garlic cloves

Zest and juice of 1 lemon

1 tablespoon (15 mL) Dijon mustard

½ teaspoon (2 mL) of your favourite hot sauce

Leaves and tender stems from 1 bunch of fresh tarragon

¼ cup (60 mL) mayonnaise

¼ cup (60 mL) extra-virgin canola or olive oil

Cucumber Radish Salad

2 English cucumbers, quartered lengthwise, cut into bite-size cubes

1 pound (450 g) red radishes, cleaned, ends trimmed, quartered

A handful of radish sprouts or other savoury, snappy fresh microgreens such as kale, radish, turnip, or cress (about 2 ounces/57 g)

chef nghe tran's goi ga (vietnamese cabbage chicken slaw)

Serves 4 as vegetable-forward meal or 8 as a side

My good friend and colleague Chef Nghe Tran brings his uniquely Vietnamese-Chinese-Canadian cooking perspective to our farm. Our families' meals together remind us that our love of fresh vegetable-forward cooking is universal. When our green cabbage and mint are at their best, Nghe often shares with us a simple goi ga, a slaw-like salad dressed with his classic nuoc cham sauce, all at once spicy, sour, sweet, and savoury. Adding a shredded lemon-braised chicken breast transforms the slaw into an entire meal for four or more.

Make the Nuoc Cham

Measure the water and sugar into a small saucepan and briefly simmer over medium heat, swirling until the sugar has dissolved into a syrup. Remove from the heat and rest until cool. Stir in the lemon zest and juice, fish sauce, vegetable oil, garlic, chilies, and one-third of the ginger matchsticks. Use immediately, rest until needed, or transfer to a resealable container and refrigerate for up to 3 days.

Make the Lemon-Braised Chicken

Position the chicken breast between two layers of plastic wrap on your work surface. Using a rolling pin, roll and flatten the chicken, tenderizing it, doubling the surface area and halving the thickness. Pour the vegetable oil into a small skillet. Position half the lemon slices in a single tight layer in the pan, sprinkle with some ginger, top with the chicken, then more ginger, and the remaining lemon slices. Pour in the water. Cover and gently simmer over medium heat until fragrant and chicken is tender, about 5 minutes. Without uncovering, remove from the heat and let sit until cool enough to handle. Discard the lemon. Use two forks to pull the chicken into shreds. Stir with the pan juices.

Make the Vietnamese Slaw

In a festive serving bowl, combine the cabbage, carrots, mint, ginger, reserved chicken with juices, and nuoc cham. Thoroughly toss together until evenly dressed.

Heat the vegetable oil in a small skillet over medium-high heat. Add the garlic, remove from the heat, and gently swirl until fragrant and golden brown, mere seconds. Immediately drizzle over the slaw.

Nuoc Cham

½ cup (125 mL) water

3 tablespoons (45 mL) jaggery, raw cane sugar, or light brown sugar

Zest and juice of 3 lemons

¼ cup (60 mL) fish sauce

1 tablespoon (15 mL) vegetable oil

2 garlic cloves, finely grated with a microplane or finely minced

2 small fresh red Thai or bird's-eye chilies, very thinly sliced

1 (2-inch/5 cm) piece unpeeled fresh ginger, cut into very fine matchsticks (two-thirds reserved, divided; see below)

Lemon-Braised Chicken

1 skinless, boneless chicken breast (about 10 ounces/280 g)

1 teaspoon (5 mL) vegetable oil

1 lemon, thinly sliced

One-third reserved ginger matchsticks (see above)

2 tablespoons (30 mL) water

Vietnamese Slaw

1 green cabbage, quartered, cored, very thinly sliced

2 carrots, peeled, cut lengthwise into 2-inch (5 cm) pieces, cut into matchsticks

Leaves and tender stems from a bunch of fresh mint, a few sprigs reserved for garnish

One-third reserved ginger matchsticks (see above)

1 tablespoon (15 mL) vegetable oil

2 garlic cloves, finely minced

bacon-steamed baby turnips and greens

A single slice of bacon, a bit of cured pancetta, or other classic cured meat is enough to lightly flavour a batch of baby turnips or other relatively bland or neutrally flavoured vegetables. This simple method uses steam to tenderize the vegetable and meat as a condiment to elevate its flavour.

Toss the bacon into a medium saucepan, skillet, or Dutch oven over medium-high heat with just a splash of water to help it cook evenly. Stir frequently until lightly browned and crispy, 5 minutes or so. Add the water and gently swirl, dissolving the browned bits from the bottom of the pan into a tasty broth. Add the turnips, cover, and steam just until tender, 5 minutes or so. Remove from the heat. Lightly season with salt and pepper.

1 slice bacon, chopped (or a few slices cured pancetta or prosciutto, chopped, and a splash of olive oil)

½ cup (125 mL) water

2 pounds (900 g) baby turnips with greens attached, washed, long roots trimmed

Sea salt

Freshly ground pepper

smoked salmon celery root brandade

caraway rye crackers

Classic brandade is a purée of salt cod with just enough potato and oil to make it creamy and smooth. In this more-vegetable-than-fish version, sweet celery root, hot-smoked salmon, and fragrant dill combine into a deliciously smooth dip ready for sharing with family and friends. Crispy crackers loaded with traditional gluten-free rye bread flavour will help you find the bottom of the bowl.

Make the Caraway Rye Crackers

Measure the rye flour, caraway seeds, baking powder, and salt into a food processor. Briefly pulse together. Add the butter and pulse to combine. Add the milk and molasses and pulse until thoroughly mixed into a smooth dough. Divide the dough in half and shape each half into a ball. Roll each ball into a tight cylinder 2 inches (5 cm) thick and about 8 inches (20 cm) long. Tightly wrap each in plastic wrap. Refrigerate until firm, at least an hour or for up to 5 days.

Arrange the oven racks in the upper and lower thirds of the oven and preheat to 350°F (180°C). Turn on the convection fan if you have one. Line 2 baking sheets with silicone baking mats or parchment paper.

Unwrap the dough. Cut each dough cylinder into thin, even slices, about ⅛ inch (3 mm) thick. Position the rounds in tight rows, evenly filling the prepared baking sheets. Bake, rotating the pans halfway through, until lightly browned and evenly cooked, 15 minutes or so. Let the crackers rest on the baking sheets until they are cool enough to handle. Use immediately or transfer to a resealable container and store at room temperature for up to 3 days.

Make the Smoked Salmon Brandade

Bring a large pot of lightly salted water to a boil over medium-high heat. Add the celery root and cook until tender, 15 minutes or so. Drain the celery root and transfer to a food processor. Add the smoked salmon, garlic, lemon zest and juice, and salt. Purée until smooth. With the machine running, pour in a steady stream of the cream and then the olive oil, processing until the mixture is combined. Stir in the dill. Taste and adjust seasoning. Use immediately or transfer to a resealable container and refrigerate for up to 3 days. Serve with caraway rye crackers for dipping.

Serves 8 to 12 as a vegetable-forward dip

Caraway Rye Crackers (makes 6 dozen)

2 cups (500 mL) rye flour

2 tablespoons (30 mL) caraway seeds

2 teaspoons (10 mL) baking powder

1 teaspoon (5 mL) sea salt

½ cup (125 mL) cold butter, cut into small cubes

½ cup (125 mL) whole milk

2 tablespoons (30 mL) fancy molasses

Smoked Salmon Celery Root Brandade (makes about 6 cups/1.5 L)

1 celery root (about 1 pound/ 450 g), peeled, rinsed, and cut into 2-inch (5 cm) cubes

8 ounces (225 g) hot-smoked salmon (not cold-smoked), broken into chunks

4 garlic cloves, finely grated with a microplane or finely minced

Zest and juice of 2 lemons

½ teaspoon (2 mL) sea salt

½ cup (125 mL) heavy (35%) cream

½ cup (125 mL) olive oil

Leaves and tender stems from 1 bunch of fresh dill, minced

corn and smoked salmon chowder

grilled corn basil relish

Serves 4 as a vegetable-forward main or 6 as a side

Shuck a dozen ears of sweet corn into two piles. Simmer half into soup and grill the rest for garnish. Add a chunk of hot-smoked salmon and a few handfuls of fresh fragrant basil to enjoy a bowl filled with the sweet taste of summer.

Make the Grilled Corn Basil Relish

Build and tend an aromatic fire in your firepit, burning down to a thick bed of glowing hot coals. Alternatively, fire up your barbecue or grill.

Lightly rub the corn, poblano pepper, bell pepper, and onion slices with vegetable oil, salt, and pepper. Grill, turning frequently, until the vegetables are tender and lightly charred, 10 minutes or so. Remove and rest until cool enough to handle. Carefully shave the kernels from the cobs, cutting into a medium bowl to contain the mess. Finely dice the poblano pepper, bell pepper, and red onion. Stir into the corn with the lime zest and juice and the basil. Reserve or transfer to a resealable container and refrigerate for up to 3 days.

Make the Corn and Smoked Salmon Chowder

Melt the butter in a medium saucepan over medium-low heat. Stir in the onion and garlic, cover, and cook, stirring frequently, until soft and fragrant but not browning, 5 minutes or so. Add the white wine, bring to a simmer, and cook until reduced by half. Stir in the milk, cream, salt, and chili flakes. Bring to a slow simmer. Add the corn kernels, cover, and cook until the corn is tender, 5 minutes or so. Transfer to a high-speed blender and carefully purée until smooth. (Hot liquids are dangerous—they can violently erupt. For safety, drape a kitchen towel over the blender, start slowly, then gradually increase the speed.) Pour into serving bowls. Nestle in a chunk of smoked salmon, top with lots of grilled corn basil relish, and garnish with reserved basil sprigs.

Grilled Corn Basil Relish

6 ears of fresh corn, shucked

1 poblano pepper, halved, stem and seeds removed

1 red bell pepper, halved, stem and seeds removed

1 red onion, cut into thick slices, rings keep intact

2 tablespoons (30 mL) vegetable oil

Sea salt

Freshly ground pepper

Zest and juice of 2 limes

Leaves from 1 bunch of fresh basil, tightly rolled and thinly sliced, 4 or 6 small sprigs reserved for garnish

Corn and Smoked Salmon Chowder

2 tablespoons (30 mL) butter

1 large white or yellow onion, finely minced

4 garlic cloves, thinly sliced

½ cup (125 mL) dry white wine

2 cups (500 mL) whole milk

1 cup (250 mL) heavy (35%) cream

1 teaspoon (5 mL) sea salt

½ teaspoon (2 mL) Red Chili Flakes (page 219) or store-bought

6 cups (1.5 L) corn kernels (from 6 ears of fresh corn)

8 ounces (225 g) hot-smoked salmon, pulled into 4 or 6 pieces

broccoli clam chowder

garlic thyme broth, cracker crumbs

Stir together the rich tradition of East Coast chowder—classically crafted with authentic bottled bar clams, lots of fragrant fresh thyme, and a garlicky broth—with untraditional bright green tender broccoli for a hearty vegetable-forward version of this classic. The rich umami flavour of the broccoli is delicious with clams. Fragrant thyme is a staple both in our indoor herb house and in our outdoor raised beds.

Melt the butter in a medium saucepan over medium-low heat. Stir in the broccoli stems and onions. Cover and cook, stirring frequently, until soft and fragrant but not browning, 5 minutes or so. Add the white wine, bring to a simmer, and cook until reduced by half. Stir in the clams, clam juice, cream, garlic, thyme, and chili flakes. Bring to a slow simmer. Top with the broccoli florets, cover, and cook, without stirring, until the broccoli is bright green, fragrant, and tender, 5 minutes or so. Evenly divide the chowder among bowls. Crumble the crackers over top.

Serves 4 to 6 as a vegetable-forward main

4 tablespoons (60 mL) butter

2 bunches of broccoli, cut into florets, tender stems finely diced

1 large white or yellow onion, finely minced

½ cup (125 mL) dry white wine

2 jars (5 ounces/153 g each) East Coast bar clams (see page 229), chopped, juices reserved

1 cup (250 mL) heavy (35%) cream

6 garlic cloves, finely grated with a microplane or finely minced

Leaves and tender stems from 8 sprigs of fresh thyme, finely minced

¼ teaspoon (1 mL) Red Chili Flakes (page 219) or store-bought

4 to 6 saltine-style crackers

potatoes and beef
baked potatoes and cracklings, beefy roast potatoes

Potatoes and beef fat are fundamentally delicious together. Empires have been built frying potatoes in beef fat to make the very best french fries. At home you can easily, inexpensively render your own beef fat, then use the flavourful fat in your cooking. Potato wedges tossed in beef fat and simply roasted are addictive, a guaranteed hit. The leftover crispy cracklings are a legendary treat for the cook and an incredible way to level up a humble baked potato.

Render the Beef Fat
Toss the beef fat and water into a medium saucepan. Bring to a slow, steady simmer over medium heat, then adjust the heat to the lowest setting and cook, stirring frequently, slowly rendering the fat. The water initially moderates the heat and will eventually evaporate. The chunks will shrink dramatically, release all their fat, and eventually lightly brown and crisp. Watch the telltale bubbles: they'll crescendo, dramatically reduce to a bare simmer, and disappear once the fat is fully rendered, 30 minutes or so. Remove from the heat. Strain through a fine-mesh strainer. Use immediately or transfer to a resealable container and refrigerate for up to 1 month. Enjoy the cracklings immediately or reserve and briefly reheat in a microwave when needed.

Baked Potatoes and Cracklings
Preheat the oven to 425°F (220°C). Turn on the convection fan if you have one.

Bake the potatoes directly on the oven rack until tender, about 1 hour. Test doneness by poking with a skewer. Remove from the oven. Slice the baked potatoes open lengthwise and season with flaky salt and pepper. Serve with butter and a handful of hot cracklings.

or

Beefy Roast Potatoes
Preheat the oven to 350°F (180°C). Turn on the convection fan if you have one.

In a large bowl, toss the potatoes with the beef fat, coarse salt, and pepper until evenly coated. Spread evenly on a baking sheet and roast, shaking, and settling the pan once or twice, until tender, golden brown, and crispy, 45 minutes or so. Remove from the oven, sprinkle with thyme, and serve with ketchup for dipping.

Makes enough baked potatoes and crackling for 4 or enough beefy roast potatoes for 4 to 6

Rendered Beef Fat (makes about 2 cups/500 mL)

2 pounds (900 g) beef fat trim, cut into small cubes

1 cup (250 mL) water

Baked Potatoes and Cracklings

4 large baking potatoes

Flaky sea salt

Freshly ground pepper

Butter, for serving

Reserved beef fat cracklings (from recipe above)

or

Beefy Roast Potatoes

2 pounds (900 g) large baking potatoes, each cut into 4 wedges

¼ cup (60 mL) reserved beef fat, melted (from recipe above)

Coarse sea salt

Freshly ground pepper

Leaves and tender stems from 3 or 4 sprigs of fresh thyme (about 1 tablespoon/15 mL)

Ketchup, for dipping

bacon, baked beans, and kale

Bacon can be strategic. Just a few slices will deeply flavour an entire batch of classic baked beans, enticing everyone to devour it. Then you can stir in the goodness of a whole head of kale and no one will complain. Give beans the time they need to soften and they'll eventually absorb enough moisture to easily wilt the durable kale. The hearty green adds lots of complementary flavour and beneficial nutrients in this fresh update of classic baked beans.

Place the beans in a medium bowl and add water to cover by a few inches. Soak overnight. Drain well.

Preheat the oven to 300°F (150°C). Turn on the convection fan if you have one.

Toss the bacon into a large flameproof casserole dish or Dutch oven over medium-high heat with just a splash of water to help it cook evenly. Stir frequently until browned and crispy, 5 minutes or so. Add the onions and garlic and cook, stirring constantly, just long enough to soften and dissolve the browned bacon bits, a minute or so. Add the drained beans, ketchup, maple syrup, mustard, and bay leaves. Stir in 4 cups (1 L) of the water. Bring to a full simmer, stirring frequently, then cover and bake for 2 hours. Stir in the remaining 2 cups (500 mL) water and continue cooking until the beans are tender, a further 2 hours or so. Remove from the oven. Stir in the Worcestershire sauce and kale, cover, and rest until the kale is bright green and wilted, 5 minutes or so.

Serves 6 to 8 as a vegetable-forward meal or 8 to 12 as a side

2 pounds (900 g) dry white beans

4 ounces (115 g) thick sliced bacon, cut crosswise into thin strips

4 yellow onions, finely diced

Cloves from 1 head of garlic, thinly sliced

1 cup (250 mL) ketchup

1 cup (250 mL) pure maple syrup

¼ cup (60 mL) dry mustard

2 bay leaves

6 cups (1.5 L) water, divided

2 tablespoons (30 mL) Worcestershire sauce

1 large bunch of kale (about 1 pound/450 g), centre ribs removed, leaves stacked, rolled up, and thinly sliced

potato, leek, mushroom, and chicken skillet stew

You don't have to roast a chicken to enjoy its full flavour—a few chicken thighs are all it takes. In this easy stew, they're browned in a pan and then stretched into a full meal with lots of complementary vegetables— earthy potatoes, sweet tender leeks, and meaty mushrooms—slowly braised with the chicken in aromatic vermouth and rich cream, then finished with sharp, bright tarragon.

Preheat the oven to 350°F (180°C). Turn on the convection fan if you have one.

Lightly season the chicken thighs with salt and pepper. Heat the vegetable oil in a large, heavy skillet over medium-high heat. Position the chicken thighs skin side down in the pan and cook, maintaining a sizzling heat as the skin releases its flavourful fat, until the skin is browned and crispy, 10 minutes or so. Turn over and continue cooking until equally browned. If the crispy skin pulls away, feel free to have a snack. Transfer the chicken pieces to a plate. Add the mushrooms to the chicken fat in the pan, gently stirring to dislodge any browned bits from the bottom of the pan, and cook until lightly browned, 5 minutes or so. Add the leeks, potatoes, garlic, vermouth, cream, and 1 teaspoon (5 mL) salt. Nestle in the chicken pieces and any accumulated juices, reduce the heat to a bare simmer, cover, and bake until the chicken is tender and the sauce has thickened, 1 hour. Remove from the oven. Stir in the tarragon at the last second, preserving its bright intensity. Serve garnished with tarragon sprigs.

Serves 4 to 6 as a vegetable-forward main

6 skin-on, bone-in chicken thighs (1½ pounds/675 g total)

1 teaspoon (5 mL) sea salt, plus more for chicken

Freshly ground pepper

1 tablespoon (15 mL) vegetable oil

1 pound (450 g) king mushrooms or other mushroom variety, halved lengthwise

2 to 3 leeks, tops and bottoms trimmed, halved lengthwise, cut into 2-inch (5 cm) pieces, rinsed well, and drained

1 pound (450 g) whole baby potatoes or quartered large potatoes

Cloves from 1 head of garlic, peeled and halved

1 cup (250 mL) dry vermouth, sherry, port, or white or red wine

1 cup (250 mL) heavy (35%) cream

Leaves and tender stems from 1 bunch of fresh tarragon, minced, 4 to 6 sprigs reserved for garnish

slow-roasted pork, poblano, fennel, and tomatoes
fennel frond dressing

The medium heat of poblano peppers balances sweet fennel, bright tomatoes, and pungent garlic, forming a delicious roasting bed for pork crusted with spice seeds. Reserved fennel fronds add bright licorice flavour to a sharp dressing that complements the slowly roasted vegetables and meat.

Serves 6 to 8 as a vegetable-forward main

Roasted Poblano, Fennel, and Tomatoes

4 poblano peppers, halved, stems and seeds removed

1 fennel bulb, trimmed, feathery fronds reserved, bulb halved, cored, and thinly sliced lengthwise

2 pints (1 L) cherry tomatoes or grape tomatoes

2 white or yellow onions, thinly sliced

Cloves from 1 head of garlic, peeled and halved

2 tablespoons (30 mL) reserved bacon fat or other reserved animal fat (see page 3), vegetable oil, or olive oil

2 tablespoons (30 mL) fennel seeds

1 tablespoon (15 mL) cumin seeds

1 teaspoon (5 mL) sea salt

Fennel Frond Dressing

½ cup (125 mL) olive oil

¼ cup (60 mL) red wine vinegar

2 anchovy fillets, drained

2 garlic cloves, sliced

1 tablespoon (15 mL) pure liquid honey

1 teaspoon (5 mL) Dijon mustard

½ teaspoon (2 mL) Red Chili Flakes (page 219) or store-bought

Reserved fennel fronds (at left)

Slow-Roasted Pork

2 bay leaves

2 tablespoons (30 mL) coriander seeds

2 tablespoons (30 mL) fennel seeds

2 tablespoons (30 mL) brown sugar

1 teaspoon (5 mL) sea salt

1 pound (450 g) boneless pork loin, trimmed and cut lengthwise into 2 or 3 long roasts, or pork tenderloins

Ready the Vegetables
Preheat the oven to 350° (180°C). Turn on the convection fan if you have one.

In a large bowl, toss together the poblanos, fennel, tomatoes, onions, garlic, bacon fat, fennel seeds, cumin seeds, and salt. Transfer to a large roasting pan. Shake and settle into a thick roasting bed ready for the pork.

Make the Fennel Frond Dressing
Measure the olive oil, red wine vinegar, anchovies, garlic, honey, mustard, and chili flakes into a food processor. Purée until smooth. Add the reserved fennel fronds and process until smooth. Reserve.

Spice-Crust and Roast the Pork
In a spice grinder or coffee grinder, combine the bay leaves, coriander seeds, fennel seeds, brown sugar, and salt and grind into a coarse powder. Toss with the pork roasts in a large bowl until fully and evenly coated. Position the pork roasts at even intervals over the vegetables and transfer to the oven. Roast, shaking and settling the pan every 15 minutes or so, until the vegetables and meat are tender and lightly browned, about 60 minutes. Turn off the heat and without opening the oven door, rest for 15 more minutes. Remove from the oven. Thinly slice the pork and return to the pan with any juices. Serve with the fennel frond dressing poured over the roast pork and vegetables.

grilled summer salad

lemon garlic yogurt dressing, miso turnip purée

Your favourite beefy grilled steak doesn't always have to be the star of the show. Instead, let it share the bill with vegetables in a warm summer salad. The firm texture of fresh summer beans works well on the grill too. Sweet bean sprouts add freshness, shiso leaves bring intriguing minty spice notes to the mix, and a humble turnip purée deliciously seasoned with miso grounds the salad.

Make the Lemon Garlic Yogurt Dressing

In a small bowl combine the yogurt, canola oil, lemon zest and juice, mustard, garlic, shallot, and salt. Whisk until smooth. Reserve or transfer to a resealable container and refrigerate for up to 3 days.

Make the Miso Turnip Purée

In a small saucepan, bring the turnip and water to a full boil over medium heat. Reduce the heat to a bare simmer, cover, and cook until tender, 20 minutes or so. Transfer the turnip and cooking water to a high-speed blender, add the miso, and carefully purée until smooth. (Hot liquids are dangerous—they can violently erupt. For safety, drape a kitchen towel over the blender, start slowly, then gradually increase the speed.) Return to the pot and reserve until needed. Reheat briefly before serving.

Make the Grilled Summer Salad

Build and tend an aromatic fire in your firepit, burning down to a thick bed of glowing hot coals. Alternatively, fire up your barbecue or grill.

Lightly oil the steak and season with salt and pepper. Grill, flipping once or twice, until medium rare and lightly charred, 15 minutes or so. Remove from the heat and rest. Lightly oil the beans and season with salt and pepper. Grill until tender and lightly charred, 5 minutes or so. Transfer to a bowl and add the bean sprouts, shiso leaves, and lemon garlic yogurt dressing. Thinly slice the rested steak and add with any accumulated juices to the beans. Lightly toss everything together to combine. Serve the grilled salad with miso turnip purée.

Serves 4 to 6 as a vegetable-forward main

Lemon Garlic Yogurt Dressing

¼ cup (60 mL) natural plain full-fat yogurt or plain Greek yogurt

¼ cup (60 mL) extra-virgin canola or olive oil

Zest and juice of 1 lemon

1 tablespoon (15 mL) Dijon mustard

2 garlic cloves, finely grated with a microplane or finely minced

1 shallot, finely minced

½ teaspoon (2 mL) sea salt

Miso Turnip Purée

1 turnip (about 1 pound/450 g), peeled and cubed

2 cups (500 mL) water

2 tablespoons (30 mL) yellow miso

Grilled Summer Salad

8-ounce (225 g) flatiron steak or your favourite grilling steak

2 tablespoons (30 mL) vegetable oil

Sea salt

Freshly ground pepper

2 pounds (900 g) summer beans, green beans, yellow beans, or romano beans, woody stems trimmed

8 ounces (225 g) mung bean sprouts or lentil sprouts

A handful or two of fresh shiso, basil, or cilantro leaves

meat and vegetables

potato-crusted smoked salmon cakes

arugula dill salad, maritime mustard pickles

These crispy smoked salmon cakes have potatoes inside and out, in their creamy filling and their crunchy crust. Tender potatoes with chunks of smoked salmon, formed into cakes, and crusted with instant potato flakes. Topped with a fresh salad of tangy arugula, fragrant fresh dill, and the gold-standard flavours of Maritime Mustard Pickles, this is a perfect dish for the win at your next brunch!

Makes 8 vegetable-forward mains

Potato-Crusted Smoked Salmon Cakes

2 pounds (900 g) Yukon Gold potatoes, peeled and quartered

Cloves from 1 head of garlic, peeled and halved

2 bay leaves

1 tablespoon (15 mL) salt

1 tablespoon (15 mL) butter

1 yellow onion, finely diced

1 egg

1 egg yolk

2 tablespoons (30 mL) whole milk

2 tablespoons (30 mL) minced fresh thyme

1 pound (450 g) hot-smoked salmon chunks or cold-smoked salmon slices

1 cup (250 mL) all-purpose flour

4 eggs, vigorously whisked

2 cups (500 mL) instant potato flakes, panko crumbs, or dry bread crumbs

¼ cup (60 mL) vegetable oil, for frying

Arugula Dill Salad

A few handfuls of arugula leaves or other tender savoury greens such as baby spinach or baby kale (about 4 ounces/115 g)

Fronds and tender stems from 1 bunch of fresh dill

1 cup (250 mL) Maritime Mustard Pickles (page 218)

Make the Potato-Crusted Smoked Salmon Cake Base

In a large pot, combine the potatoes, garlic, bay leaves, and salt. Cover with an inch or so of water and bring to a full simmer over high heat. Reduce the heat to maintain a simmer and cook until the potatoes are tender, 15 minutes or so. Drain well. Cool completely before returning to the pot.

Meanwhile, melt the butter in a small skillet over medium heat. Toss in the onion and cook, stirring frequently, until lightly browned and fragrant. Remove from the heat.

In a medium bowl whisk together the egg, egg yolk, milk, and thyme. Add to the cooked potatoes along with the sautéed onions. Using a potato masher, mash the mixture together. Stir in the smoked salmon. Cover tightly with plastic wrap and refrigerate until cold and firm, at least 2 hours.

recipe continues

Form, Bread, and Fry the Potato-Crusted Smoked Salmon Cakes

Preheat the oven to 200°F (100°C).

Evenly divide the salmon mixture into 8 portions and use your hands to gently form into cakes about 2 inches (5 cm) thick. To keep firm, arrange on a large plate or baking sheet and place in the freezer while prepping the breading ingredients.

Place the flour, whisked eggs, and potato flakes in 3 separate shallow bowls. To minimize the mess of breaded fingers, use one hand exclusively to handle the potato cakes while they are dry with flour or potato flakes and the other while they are wet with egg. Working with one potato cake at a time, gently dredge in the flour, dusting off excess. Thoroughly dip through the eggs, draining off excess liquid. Lastly, give them a roll through the potato flakes.

Heat a large non-stick skillet over medium heat. Pour in the vegetable oil. When it's sizzling hot, carefully add the potato cakes, in batches as needed, and slowly, patiently brown them. Keep the pan sizzling gently and turn the cakes occasionally until they are evenly crisped and thoroughly cooked, about 15 minutes in total. Transfer the finished cakes to a baking sheet and keep warm in the oven for a few minutes until ready to serve.

Make the Arugula Dill Salad

Toss together the arugula and dill in a medium bowl. Add the maritime mustard pickles and gently toss to evenly dress.

Serve the potato-crusted smoked salmon cakes topped with the arugula dill salad.

beefy vegetable stew

farmhouse beef broth

You don't need to eat protein-rich beef to enjoy its full flavour. Instead, you can preserve its nutrients by simmering its goodness into a hearty broth, then cook a simple vegetable stew. All the flavour but none of the heaviness—and lots of leftover broth for your next soup, stew, or noodle bowl. The strategy is simple: cook each ingredient as much as needed to extract its flavour, but not too much to damage it.

Serves 4 as a vegetable-forward main or 8 as a side

Farmhouse Beef Broth (makes 4 quarts/4 L)

5 pounds (2.25 kg) beef shanks, oxtail, or meaty neck bones, cut crosswise into 1 to 2-inch (2.5 to 5 cm) pieces

8 cups (2 L) water, divided

4 yellow onions, thinly sliced

4 carrots, peeled and thinly sliced

4 celery stalks, thinly sliced

Cloves from 2 heads of garlic, peeled

1 can (28 ounces/796 mL) whole tomatoes in juice

1 bottle (25 ounces/750 mL) full-bodied red wine

4 bay leaves

1 teaspoon (5 mL) sea salt

Freshly ground pepper

A handful of fresh rosemary sprigs

A handful of fresh thyme sprigs

Beefy Vegetable Stew

2 tablespoons (30 mL) reserved or rendered beef fat (see page 163) or vegetable oil

2 carrots, peeled and cut into bite-size pieces

2 parsnips, peeled and cut into bite-size pieces

1 turnip, peeled and cut into bite-size pieces

1 teaspoon (5 mL) sea salt

1 pound (450 g) baby potatoes

1 leek, top and bottom trimmed, washed, sliced into 1-inch (2.5 cm) rounds

Cloves from 1 head of garlic, thinly sliced

6 to 8 cups (1.5 to 2 L) Farmhouse Beef Broth (at left)

A sprig or two of your favourite fresh finishing herbs (such as thyme, tarragon, sage, savory, rosemary, oregano, or lovage), lightly minced

2 cups (500 mL) of your favourite green vegetables (such as peas, edamame, broccoli florets, shredded kale, green beans, or baby spinach)

Sea salt

A handful of lightly minced parsley sprigs, green onions, tarragon, thyme, rosemary, or oregano

Make the Farmhouse Beef Broth

Preheat the oven to 425°F (220°C). Turn on the convection fan if you have one.

Form a single layer of beef pieces in a large roasting pan. Roast, shaking and settling the pan occasionally, turning the pieces as they cook, until deliciously browned and evenly caramelized, 30 minutes or so. Transfer the beef to a large stock pot. Pour 2 cups (500 mL) of the water into the roasting pan. Rest until the flavourful browned bits on the bottom are loosened, then stir and scrape the contents into the pot. Add the onions, carrots, celery, garlic, tomatoes, red wine, bay leaves, salt, and pepper. Pour in the remaining 6 cups (1.5 L) water. Bring to a full boil over high heat, then reduce the heat to a slow, steady simmer, cover, and simmer for 3 full hours. Remove from the heat, stir in the rosemary and thyme sprigs, cover, and rest for 1 to 2 hours more.

recipe continues

Strain the broth through a fine-mesh strainer or colander lined with several layers of cheesecloth positioned over another large pot or deep bowl, firmly pressing until fully drained. Discard the strained scraps. A thin flavourful layer of fat will form on the top of the broth—feel free to keep or discard. Reserve or transfer to a resealable container and refrigerate for up to 5 days or freeze for up to 6 months.

Make the Beefy Vegetable Stew

Add the beef fat, carrots, parsnips, turnip, and salt to a large pot. Cook over medium-high heat, stirring frequently, until lightly browned and fragrant, 10 minutes or so. Add the potatoes, leek, garlic, and farmhouse beef broth. Bring to a full boil, then reduce the heat to a slow, steady simmer, cover, and cook, without stirring, until the vegetables are tender, 20 minutes or so. Gently stir in the finishing herbs and green vegetables and cook until tender, a few minutes or more, depending on your choice. Taste and adjust seasoning with salt as needed. Remove from the heat and stir in the parsley.

roast eggplant-wrapped salmon

tomato garlic mash

Serves 4 as a vegetable-forward main

Roasting eggplant magically transforms its texture from soft and spongy to juicy and supple and releases deliciously caramelized juices. In this recipe, the eggplant slices also protect the salmon from the fierce heat of the broiler. Tomatoes and garlic, their flavours deepened by slowly roasting, are mashed into an impromptu condiment, the whole dish finished with a scattering of fresh basil and mint leaves.

Make the Tomato Garlic Mash

Preheat the oven to 350°F (180°C). Turn on the convection fan if you have one.

Measure the tomatoes, garlic, olive oil, red wine vinegar, fennel seeds, salt, and chili flakes into a large baking pan or large ovenproof skillet. Lightly toss everything together to evenly combine. Roast until the tomatoes are tender and fragrant, 45 minutes or so. Remove from the oven and rest until cool. Lightly mash and stir together with a potato masher or the back of a wooden spoon. Cover with foil and reserve until ready to serve, or transfer to a resealable container and refrigerate for up to 3 days.

Make the Roast Eggplant-Wrapped Salmon

Increase the oven temperature to 425°F (220°C). Line a baking sheet with a silicone baking mat or parchment paper.

Lay 2 eggplant slices on a work surface, overlapping them lengthwise so they are as wide together as the fish fillets are long. Lightly season with salt and pepper. Position a salmon fillet across a short edge and lightly season with salt and pepper. Roll tightly, firmly wrapping the fish. Transfer to the prepared baking sheet, positioning seam side down to tightly seal. Repeat with the remaining eggplant and salmon. Lightly season with salt and pepper and evenly brush with olive oil. Roast until the eggplant is lightly browned and the fish is cooked through, 15 minutes or so. The salmon is done when a digital or quick-read thermometer registers at least 145°F (63°C) in the thickest part. Remove from the oven. Serve topped with the tomato garlic mash and a scattering of fresh basil and mint leaves.

Tomato Garlic Mash

2 pints (1 L) cherry tomatoes or grape tomatoes, halved

Cloves from 1 head of garlic, peeled and halved

2 tablespoons (30 mL) olive oil

2 tablespoons (30 mL) red wine vinegar

1 tablespoon (15 mL) fennel seeds

1 teaspoon (5 mL) sea salt

½ teaspoon (2 mL) Red Chili Flakes (page 219) or store-bought

Roast Eggplant-Wrapped Salmon

1 large globe or Italian eggplant, ends trimmed, thinly cut lengthwise with a mandoline or sharp knife to yield 8 slices

Sea salt

Freshly ground pepper

4 skinless, boneless salmon fillets (about 1½ pounds/ 675 g total)

¼ cup (60 mL) olive oil

A handful of various fresh basil leaves

A handful of fresh mint leaves

root vegetable and roast chicken pan stew

You can roast any chicken over a big pile of vegetables, securely knowing that everything will cook safely, nothing will be lost, and much will be found. As the chicken roasts, its juices season the vegetables, helping them roast too. The roasted meat is easily shredded and stirred into a simple pan stew. This is one of the most delicious ways I know to cook meat and vegetables together.

Preheat the oven to 425°F (220°C). Turn on the convection fan if you have one.

Fill a large roasting pan with the carrots, parsnips, turnip, celery root, potatoes, leeks, and garlic. Lightly season the vegetables with salt and pepper and gently mix together. Thoroughly season the chicken with salt and pepper and nestle breast side up in the centre of the vegetables. Position the lemon halves cut side up around the chicken. Roast, gently shaking and settling the pan once or twice, until the vegetables are tender and caramelized and the chicken is golden brown and finished, an hour or so. The chicken is done when a digital or quick-read thermometer registers at least 165°F (74°C) in the thickest part of the breast meat and thigh. Remove from the oven.

With the chicken still in the pan and a pair of tongs in each hand, pull, tug, and shred the meat away from the carcass. Share the crispy skin treat with all assembled. Sprinkle with fresh herbs and squeeze the roasted lemons with a pair of tongs, allowing the juices to mingle. Stir in the greens and rest as they wilt before serving, a minute or two. Reserve the carcass for another day's chicken broth.

Serves 4 to 6 as a vegetable-forward main

2 carrots, peeled and cut into bite-size pieces

2 parsnips, peeled and cut into bite-size pieces

1 turnip, peeled and cut into bite-size pieces

1 celery root, peeled and cut into bite-size pieces

1 pound (450 g) baby potatoes

1 leek, top and bottom trimmed, cut into 2-inch (5 cm) intact rounds, rinsed as needed

Cloves from 1 head of garlic, peeled and halved

Sea salt

Freshly ground pepper

1 large roasting chicken (about 5 pounds/2.25 kg)

2 lemons, halved crosswise

Leaves from a handful of fresh rosemary, thyme, sage, savory, or oregano sprigs, minced

A few handfuls of tender savoury greens (baby spinach, baby kale, arugula, or Swiss chard)

melted cabbage, turnip, and ham hock

With time on your side, it doesn't take much effort to stuff a pot full of flavour and let the inevitability of simply, slowly baking work its magic. As cabbage cooks it releases moisture, forming a savoury broth with the smoked ham hock, and melting into a tender, meaty texture of its own that perfectly soaks up the surrounding meaty broth. Deliciously symbiotic!

Preheat the oven to 300°F (150°C). Turn on the convection fan if you have one.

Fill a large pot or Dutch oven with the ham hock, cabbage, turnip, water, white wine, mustard, honey, and caraway seeds. Bring to a full furious boil over medium-high heat. Remove from the heat, shake and settle the pot, cover, transfer to the oven, and bake until meltingly tender, 3 hours. Taste the broth and adjust seasoning with salt as needed. Remove the ham hock and discard the skin, fat, and bone pieces. Break the meat into large chunks and serve with the cabbage broth.

Serves 6 to 8 as a vegetable-forward main

1 smoked ham hock (about 3 pounds/1.35 kg)

1 cabbage, quartered, cored, and thinly sliced

1 turnip, peeled and diced

3 cups (750 mL) water

1 cup (250 mL) dry white wine

½ cup (125 mL) grainy mustard

¼ cup (60 mL) pure liquid honey

1 tablespoon (15 mL) caraway seeds

Sea salt

slow-roasted duck and winter vegetables

rosemary roasted applesauce

A richly flavoured duck, slowly roasted over a bed of firm vegetables and soft apples, eventually tenderizes into a delicious meal in just one pan. It takes more time than thyme, though, and rosemary helps too. Unlike chicken, duck benefits from prolonged cooking, and mellow rosemary can handle the long, slow ride too. The sauce makes itself along the way. Roasted apples melt into an aromatic sauce to be stirred up with the vegetables, duck, and its flavourful drippings.

Preheat the oven to 300°F (150°C). Turn on the convection fan if you have one.

Fill a large roasting pan with the vegetables, apples, garlic, and rosemary. Season with salt and pepper and gently and thoroughly mix together. Thoroughly season the duck with salt and nestle breast side up in the centre of the vegetables. Roast, gently shaking and settling the pan once or twice, until the vegetables are tender and caramelized and the duck is golden brown and meltingly tender, 3½ hours. Remove from the oven, cover with foil, and rest for 30 minutes.

With the duck still in the pan and a pair of tongs in each hand, pull, tug, and shred the meat away from the carcass. Discard the carcass. Share the crispy skin treat with all assembled. Lightly stir the meat into the vegetables in the pan, allowing the softer apples to melt around the firmer vegetables.

Serves 4 to 6 as a vegetable-forward main

5 pounds (2.25 kg) or so of assorted winter squashes and roots (potatoes, turnips, parsnips, carrots, celery root, butternut squash, acorn squash, or sweet potato), peeled and cut into bite-size pieces

6 large Honeycrisp apples (about 1 pound/450 g) or other tart, crisp apple, cored and quartered

Cloves from 1 head of garlic, peeled and halved

Leaves from 6 large sprigs of fresh rosemary, finely minced

1 teaspoon (5 mL) sea salt

Freshly ground pepper

1 duck (about 5 pounds/ 2.25 kg), untied

pan-roasted cauliflower, leek, apple, and cinnamon-crusted pork tenderloin

It's easy to fit an entire meal in a pan when you roast your favourite meat over a bed of vegetables. This simple method is infinitely adaptable to the contents of your fridge and the harvest of the day. Simplicity is the goal and just about anything goes. Here, cauliflower, leeks, and apples slowly roast, absorbing the juices and flavours of cinnamon-crusted pork tenderloin. The toughest part is leaving leftovers!

Preheat the oven to 350°F (180°C). Turn on the convection fan if you have one.

In a large roasting pan, gently toss together the cauliflower, leeks, apples, cumin seeds, coriander seeds, and vegetable oil. Lightly season with salt and pepper.

In a medium bowl, whisk together the brown sugar, cinnamon, salt, and pepper. Roll the pork tenderloin in the mixture to evenly coat. Nestle the pork in the centre of the vegetables. Roast, gently shaking and settling the pan once or twice, until the vegetables and pork are tender and lightly browned, 45 minutes or so. The pork is done when a digital or quick-read thermometer registers at least 145°F (63°C) in the thickest part of the meat. Remove from the oven and rest a few minutes. Thinly slice the pork and return it to the pan with any accumulated juices. Stir together gently before serving.

Serves 4 to 6 as a vegetable-forward main

Pan-Roasted Vegetables

1 head of cauliflower, cut into small florets, stem diced

1 bunch of leeks, tops and bottoms trimmed, cut into 2-inch (5 cm) intact rounds, rinsed as needed

4 Honeycrisp apples or your favourite apple (about 1 pound/450 g), cored and quartered

1 tablespoon (15 mL) cumin seeds

1 tablespoon (15 mL) coriander seeds

1 tablespoon (15 mL) vegetable oil, bacon drippings, or other reserved animal fat (see page 3)

Sea salt

Freshly ground pepper

Cinnamon-Crusted Pork Tenderloin

¼ cup (60 mL) firmly packed brown sugar

1 tablespoon (15 mL) cinnamon

1 teaspoon (5 mL) sea salt

Freshly ground pepper

1 pork tenderloin (about 1 pound/450 g), tough silverskin removed

farmhouse sips and treats

tomato lillet splash

marigold ice cubes

When tomatoes are at the very peak of their sunny summer ripeness, you can purée the fragrant fruit to release a stunningly flavourful golden nectar. Tomato water is strained from the red pulp, crystal clear and incredibly aromatic. Splash in Lillet Blanc, the classic French floral-herbal aperitif, for complementary perfume and pleasingly balanced bitter notes. Marigolds are companion-planted with tomatoes on our organic farm; their scent is irritating to pests that adore tomatoes but delicious to us. Cleverly suspended in ice, they're just the right garnish.

Make the Marigold Ice Cubes

Fill an ice cube tray or large ice moulds about halfway with water. Add a few marigold flowers to each compartment. Freeze until solid, at least 2 hours. The flowers will float a bit above the water. Level the tops with a splash more water and freeze until solid yet again, 2 more hours. Store in the freezer for up to 1 week.

Make Tomato Water (makes about 3 quarts/3 L)

Line a large sieve set over a stock pot with 4 large layers of cheesecloth.

Half fill a high-speed blender with tomatoes. Purée until very smooth. Add more tomatoes, filling the blender, season with some of the salt, and purée until smooth. Pour the purée into the cloth-lined sieve. Repeat with the remaining tomatoes and salt.

Without squeezing the purée, gather the sides of the cheesecloth together, forming a bag, and tie the neck tightly with string. Tie the sack to a wooden spoon, stick, or ruler wider than the pot and remove the sieve. Suspend the sack in the pot, leaving enough room under the sack so it will not sit in the accumulated tomato water. Do not squeeze the bag or the tomato water will be cloudy. Make room in your refrigerator and hang overnight as the clear golden nectar fully drains. Use immediately or transfer to a resealable container and refrigerate for up to 1 week.

Craft the Cocktail

Place a few marigold ice cubes in each cocktail glass. Add 2 ounces of the Lillet Blanc and top with ½ cup (125 mL) of the tomato water. Garnish with a few marigold flowers and fresh basil sprigs.

Marigold Ice Cubes
A handful of freshly picked marigold flowers

Tomato Lillet Splash
5 pounds (2.25 kg) juicy ripe tomatoes (choose varieties with high moisture content, avoiding fleshier Roma or plum types), halved

1 tablespoon (15 mL) sea salt

8 ounces Lillet Blanc

8 sprigs of fresh basil

herb house lemonade

lemon verbena, lemon balm, lemon thyme, local moonshine

Our herb house and herb garden are full of various citrus-flavoured herbs, many with particularly lemony flavours. We infuse our favourites into old-school lemonade to add a refreshing boost to this classic hot-summer-day treat. If some locally distilled spirit splashes in too, all the better. A touch of salt adds pitch-perfect savoury balance that you'll instantly crave in every lemonade from now on!

Make the Lemonade
Pour 2 cups (500 mL) of the water and sugar into a small saucepan and bring to a steady simmer over medium-high heat. Stir in the lemon thyme, remove from the heat, cover, and steep for an hour or so, infusing the syrup with strong citrus flavour. Discard the thyme sprigs. Pour and scrape every drop of the syrup into an 8-cup (2 L) jar or festive jug. Stir in the remaining 5 cups (1.25 L) water, lemon verbena, lemon mint, lemon balm, lemon zest and juice, and salt. Cover tightly and refrigerate overnight to fully infuse the citrus flavours. Keep refrigerated for up to 1 week.

Craft the Cocktail
Fill tall festive glasses with ice cubes. Pour in an ounce or so of vodka into each glass and top with lemonade, holding back the infused herbs with a spoon as you pour. Garnish with a few fresh herb sprigs.

Makes 8 cups (2 L) lemonade, enough for 8 cocktails

7 cups (1.65 L) tap water

1 cup (250 mL) sugar

A large handful of fresh lemon thyme sprigs

A large handful of fresh lemon verbena sprigs

A large handful of fresh lemon mint sprigs

A large handful of fresh lemon balm sprigs

Zest and juice of 12 lemons

1 teaspoon (5 mL) sea salt

Ice cubes

8 ounces locally distilled vodka (see page 229) or your favourite vodka

A few fresh lemony herb sprigs (of any type above), for garnish

cucumber gin ice pops

borage blossom confetti

So often similar flavours are found growing separately on our farm. Our various crisp cucumbers and ubiquitous borage share a distinctive floral fragrance with the herb salad burnet. Gin is a part of the family too, as it's often infused with these very flavours. In this fun yet grown-up summer treat, each plays its role perfectly.

Tear the colourful petals from half of the borage flowers and place in a very small bowl. Reserve the remaining whole blossoms.

Measure the water and sugar into a small saucepan. Swirling gently, bring to a full simmer over medium heat. Remove from the heat and rest until cool. In a medium bowl, stir together the cucumber purée, gin, and lime juice. Add every drop of the syrup and stir until smooth. Evenly divide the whole borage blossoms among ice pop moulds and fill with the purée mixture. Freeze until rock solid, at least 4 hours, better overnight.

With the tip of the frozen mould pointing down, briefly hold the mould under a stream of hot running water, just long enough to release the treat within mere seconds. Dip the sticky frozen tip of the ice pop in the bowl of reserved borage petals and share immediately. The ice pops will stay fresh for 1 week in the freezer.

Makes 4 large or 8 small ice pops

A handful of fresh borage blossoms

¼ cup (60 mL) water

⅓ cup (75 mL) sugar

2 large English cucumbers, peeled, seeded, and puréed (2 cups/500 mL purée)

2 ounces of your favourite gin

2 tablespoons (30 mL) freshly squeezed lime juice

"anne's mistake" raspberry cordial

Prince Edward Island wasn't the only place that knew how to preserve fresh fruit, with or without local spirits, nor was Anne the only kid to crave the fresh flavour of summer's best in a sweet raspberry treat. She got it wrong that day, but you can get it right today. The innocent cordial syrup of the story was left behind in the cellar, but the recipe is in your hands now. Whether you enjoy it straight up as Anne hoped to serve it, or splash in fragrant gin and toast her with a cocktail, is up to you. Cheers!

Make the Raspberry Ice Cubes
Divide the raspberries evenly among 16 large ice cube moulds or 32 standard ice cube moulds. Fill the compartments with water and freeze solid. Store in the freezer for up to 1 week.

Make the Raspberry Cordial Syrup
Pour the water, sugar, and lemon zest and juice into a large saucepan. Bring to a full simmer over medium-high heat. Remove from the heat. Gently stir in the raspberries, cover, and refrigerate for 24 hours.

Pour the raspberry mixture through a fine-mesh sieve, pressing gently to minimize sediment, patiently draining every flavourful drop. Transfer the syrup to a glass jar or bottle. Use immediately or refrigerate for up to 5 days.

Craft the Cocktail
Fill a festive glass with raspberry ice cubes. Pour in the raspberry cordial syrup and gin. Top with tonic water, stir gently, and garnish with a mint sprig.

Makes enough raspberry cordial syrup for 12 cocktails

Raspberry Ice Cubes

1 pint (2 cups/500 mL) fresh raspberries

Raspberry Cordial Syrup (makes 6 cups/1.5 L)

2 cups (500 mL) water

2 cups (500 mL) sugar

Zest and juice of 2 large lemons

2 pounds (900 g) fresh raspberries

For each Raspberry Cordial Cocktail

½ cup (125 mL) Raspberry Cordial Syrup (recipe above)

1 ounce or so of your favourite gin

⅔ cup (150 mL) tonic water

A sprig of fresh mint

ice cream sandwiches

carrot cake cookies, parsnip ice cream

This delicious treat elevates the classic flavours of carrot cake in the cookies of a creamy ice cream sandwich with a surprising twist: parsnips make delicious ice cream! The light, earthy flavour of the root vegetable is distinct yet neutral, and its soft texture blends easily into the creamy ice cream base.

Makes 8 large or 12 small ice cream sandwiches

Parsnip Ice Cream

2 cups (500 mL) whole milk

2 cups (500 mL) heavy (35%) cream

4 cups (1 L) peeled and shredded parsnips (1½ pounds/675 g)

1 tablespoon (15 mL) pure vanilla extract

8 large egg yolks

1 cup (250 mL) white sugar

¼ teaspoon (1 mL) sea salt

Carrot Cake Cookies

1 cup (250 mL) all-purpose flour

1 teaspoon (5 mL) cinnamon

½ teaspoon (2 mL) ground cloves

½ teaspoon (2 mL) ground nutmeg

½ teaspoon (2 mL) ground allspice

½ teaspoon (2 mL) baking powder

½ teaspoon (2 mL) baking soda

¼ teaspoon (1 mL) sea salt

¾ cup (175 mL) butter

¾ cup (175 mL) packed brown sugar

1 teaspoon (5 mL) pure vanilla extract

1 egg

1 cup (250 mL) grated carrots

1 cup (250 mL) old-fashioned rolled oats

¼ cup (60 mL) dark raisins

Make the Parsnip Ice Cream

Measure the milk, cream, and parsnips into a large saucepan. Bring to a full simmer over medium-high heat. Cover tightly, remove from the heat, and rest until the earthy vegetable's flavours infuse the liquid, 1 hour or so.

Strain the mixture through a fine-mesh strainer into a large bowl, pressing firmly to fully extract the flavourful liquid. Discard the parsnips. Return the liquid to the saucepan. Stir in the vanilla and bring to a slow, steady simmer over medium heat.

Meanwhile, in a medium bowl, whisk together the egg yolks and white sugar. Gradually raise the temperature of the egg mixture by slowly ladling a cup or so of the hot milk mixture over them, whisking constantly as you do. Repeat with a second cup of hot milk. Transfer the warm egg mixture to the remaining milk in the saucepan, whisking as you do. Continue cooking over medium heat, stirring constantly with a rubber spatula or wooden spoon, just until the mixture thickens and coats the back of the spoon, a few minutes. Remove from the heat and stir in the salt. Pour the mixture into a resealable container and refrigerate until thoroughly chilled, at least 4 hours.

Transfer the mixture to an ice-cream maker and process according to the manufacturer's instructions. Transfer to a resealable container and freeze until set, at least 4 hours. Store in the freezer for up to 1 week.

recipe continues

Bake the Carrot Cake Cookies

Arrange the racks in the upper and lower thirds of the oven and preheat to 350°F (160°C). Turn on the convection fan if you have one. Line 2 baking sheets with silicone baking mats or parchment paper.

In a medium bowl, whisk together the flour, cinnamon, cloves, nutmeg, allspice, baking powder, baking soda, and salt.

Toss the butter into a small saucepan over medium-high heat. Swirl gently as it melts, steams, foams, and eventually lightly browns. Remove from the heat, pour into a medium bowl, and with a whisk, stir in the brown sugar and vanilla until smooth. Whisk in the egg. Add the dry ingredients to the wet ingredients, switch to a wooden spoon, and stir into a smooth batter. Thoroughly stir in the carrots, oats, and raisins.

Evenly portion spoonfuls of batter (16 portions for large cookies or 24 portions for small cookies) on the prepared baking sheets. Bake until golden brown and crispy on the bottom, 20 minutes. Remove from the oven and rest on the baking sheets until cool.

Make the Ice Cream Sandwiches

Lay half of the cookies, upside down, on your work surface. Scoop some of the parsnip ice cream onto each cookie and flatten it a bit with the back of the spoon, leaving a ½-inch (1 cm) border around the edge. Sandwich with the remaining cookies, pressing down lightly to form an even disc of ice cream. Serve immediately, or wrap tightly in plastic wrap and freeze until firm, or store in the freezer for up to 1 month.

strawberry rhubarb pavlova
lavender cream

The classic pavlova formula is simple: a base of simultaneously crispy yet magically chewy meringue, bright sweet and sour fruit filling, topped with mounds of whipped cream. This sublime dessert is its best with sweet strawberries balancing tart rhubarb, and fresh lavender fragrance cleverly infused in the whipped cream.

Infuse the Lavender Cream
Reserve half the lavender sprigs for the cream. Strip the individual flowers from the remaining sprigs, reserving the bare stems for the cream and the flowers for garnish.

In a small saucepan over low heat, gently warm the cream, honey, whole lavender sprigs, and reserved bare stems just to a bare simmer, until infused with flavour, 5 minutes or so. Stir in the vanilla, transfer to a mason jar or other resealable container, and refrigerate overnight.

Make the Strawberry Rhubarb Compote
Measure the rhubarb, white sugar, and wine into a large saucepan. Bring to a full boil over medium-high heat, stirring occasionally, then immediately reduce the heat to a slow, steady simmer. Cook until the rhubarb softens and breaks down and the liquid is reduced by two-thirds or so to a syrup, 15 minutes or so. Cool completely, then stir in the strawberries. Reserve or transfer to a resealable container and refrigerate for up to 5 days.

recipe continues

Lavender Cream

A handful of fresh lavender sprigs

2 cups (500 mL) heavy (35%) cream

1 tablespoon (15 mL) pure liquid honey

1 teaspoon (5 mL) pure vanilla extract

Strawberry Rhubarb Compote

8 ounces (225 g) fresh rhubarb, cut into 1-inch (2.5 cm) chunks

¼ cup (60 mL) white sugar

1 cup (250 mL) of your favourite red or white wine

8 ounces (225 g) fresh strawberries, hulled and halved

Meringue

6 egg whites

1 teaspoon (5 mL) pure vanilla extract

½ teaspoon (2 mL) cream of tartar

Pinch of sea salt

1½ cups (375 mL) icing sugar

1 tablespoon (15 mL) cornstarch

1 teaspoon (5 mL) white wine vinegar

Make the Meringue

Preheat the oven to 350°F (180°C). Turn on the convection fan if you have one. Line a baking sheet with a sheet of parchment paper. The parchment must lie flat inside the baking sheet, so trim if necessary. Trace a 12-inch (30 cm) circle on the parchment with a pencil. Flip over the parchment to prevent the pencil marks from transferring to your meringue.

In the bowl of a stand mixer fitted with the whisk attachment, combine the egg whites, vanilla, cream of tartar, and salt. Begin beating at low speed, increasing to high, until satiny smooth peaks form. With the machine running at low speed, add the icing sugar slowly along one side of the bowl until fully incorporated. Increase the speed and continue whipping until glossy, stiff peaks form. Sprinkle in cornstarch and vinegar and gently fold in by hand with a rubber spatula.

Gently spread the meringue inside the circle on the parchment, carefully levelling the meringue into a thick, even disc. Transfer to the oven and immediately reduce the heat to 300°F (150°C). Bake for 1 hour and 15 minutes. Turn off the oven and, without opening the door, leave the meringue until completely cooled, 2 full hours.

Whip the Lavender Cream

Strain the infused lavender cream, discarding the lavender. Whip the cream until thick.

Assemble the Pavlova

Carefully lift and peel the meringue from the parchment paper. Transfer to a festive platter. Crack the top to form a nest in the centre. Fill with the strawberry rhubarb compote. Top with a mound of lavender whipped cream. Sprinkle the reserved lavender flowers over the whipped cream.

jalapeño chocolate chip cookies

This recipe enlivens the classic cookie with not just the spicy heat of a jalapeño but its strong fragrance too. A chili's flavours are among the most aromatic on our farm. You'll find the spicy heat of these cookies initially surprising and curiously addictive. The spicy chilies accent the rich familiar flavours of the chocolate while adding lots of jalapeño flavour!

Arrange the racks in the lower and upper thirds of the oven and preheat to 350°F (180°C). Turn on the convection fan if you have one. Line 2 baking sheets with silicone baking mats or parchment paper.

In a medium bowl, whisk together the flour, baking soda, and salt. Measure the butter, white sugar, and brown sugar into the bowl of a stand mixer fitted with the whip attachment and, starting slowly then increasing speed, whip until smooth and creamy, scraping down the sides occasionally, 5 minutes or so. Stop the machine, add the eggs and vanilla, and whisk until smooth. Change to the paddle attachment, add the flour mixture, and stir into a smooth batter. Add the jalapeños and chocolate chips and slowly stir until evenly mixed.

Divide the dough into 24 portions. Using your hands, roll each piece of dough into an even ball. Place 12 dough balls on a prepared baking sheet evenly spaced, and press gently to anchor in place. Repeat with the remaining 12 dough balls, evenly spaced on the second sheet to allow for spread. Bake until tender and chewy, exactly 12 minutes. Transfer to racks and rest until cool. Store in a resealable container at room temperature for up to 3 days.

2½ cups (625 mL) all-purpose flour

1 teaspoon (5 mL) baking soda

1 teaspoon (5 mL) sea salt

1 cup (250 mL) butter, softened

1 cup (250 mL) white sugar

½ cup (125 mL) packed brown sugar

2 eggs

1 tablespoon (15 mL) pure vanilla extract

4 jalapeño peppers, halved, stems and seeds removed, finely minced

2 cups (500 mL) dark chocolate chips

old-school rhubarb

tarragon sugar

Here's a classic kitchen-garden treat: intensely tart raw rhubarb stalks dredged in balancing sugar mixed with the added fragrance of surprisingly complementary tarragon. These distinct flavours harmoniously blend into an intensely delicious delicacy best enjoyed with your fingers. Discerning garden foragers choose younger tender rhubarb, before its texture strengthens and toughens later in its life cycle.

Measure the sugar into the bowl of a small food processor. Add the tarragon and process until bright green and finely chopped. Transfer to a small festive bowl.

Share with tender rhubarb stalks, scooping up the fragrant sugar with the crisp stalks.

Makes enough for 4 to 6 to share

1 cup (250 mL) sugar

Leaves and tender stems from 1 bunch of fresh tarragon

A handful of young tender rhubarb stalks, ideally ½ to 1-inch (1 to 2.5 cm) in diameter (the thinner the better)

sweet corn fritters

tarragon blueberry stew, maple crème fraîche

Makes 12 or so fritters, enough for 4 to 6

Sweet corn is an excellent dessert ingredient. Here, crispy corn fritters are served with maple blueberry stew intriguingly accented with bright tarragon and topped with tangy, rich, maple-sweetened crème fraîche.

Make the Tarragon Blueberry Stew

Toss the blueberries, maple syrup, and lemon zest and juice into a medium saucepan. Bring to a slow, steady simmer over medium heat and cook, stirring occasionally, until thickened and reduced by half, 15 minutes or so. Remove from the heat and stir in the tarragon. Reserve, reheating briefly before serving, or rest until cool, transfer to a resealable container, and refrigerate for up to 1 week.

Make the Sweet Corn Fritter Batter

In a medium bowl, whisk together the cornmeal, sugar, baking powder, and salt, evenly distributing the finer powders amidst the coarser ones. In a high-speed blender, purée the milk, egg, and 1 cup (250 mL) of the corn kernels until smooth. Pour every drop into the dry ingredients. With a wooden spoon, stir into a smooth batter. Stir in the remaining 1 cup (250 mL) corn kernels. Cover tightly and refrigerate for 1 hour, allowing the cornmeal to hydrate and soften.

Make the Maple Crème Fraîche

Combine the cream, crème fraîche, maple syrup, and vanilla and beat until smooth and thick, 2 to 3 minutes. Use immediately or transfer to a resealable container and refrigerate until needed, a few hours.

Deep-Fry the Sweet Corn Fritters

Heat the vegetable oil in a large pot or deep-fryer over medium-high heat until it reaches 375°F (190°C) on a deep-fat thermometer. Using 2 spoons, the first to scoop, the second to release the batter, carefully drop spoonfuls of the fritter batter into the hot oil. Work in batches so you don't crowd the pot. Adjust the heat to maintain the ideal frying temperature of 365°F (185°C). Fry, stirring gently with a skimmer or slotted spoon, until golden brown and crispy, 3 to 4 minutes. Drain briefly on paper towel. (Cool, strain, and refrigerate the frying oil so you can use it again.)

Serve the sweet corn fritters with a ladleful of tarragon blueberry stew and a generous dollop of maple crème fraîche. Garnish with the reserved tarragon sprigs.

Tarragon Blueberry Stew

4 cups (1 L) fresh or frozen wild blueberries

1 cup (250 mL) pure maple syrup

Zest and juice of 1 lemon

Leaves and tender stems from 1 bunch of fresh tarragon, lightly chopped, a few sprigs reserved for garnish

Sweet Corn Fritters

1 cup (250 mL) finely ground cornmeal

1 tablespoon (15 mL) sugar

1 teaspoon (5 mL) baking powder

¼ teaspoon (1 mL) sea salt

½ cup (125 mL) whole milk

1 egg

2 cups (500 mL) fresh or frozen corn kernels, divided

8 cups (2 L) vegetable oil, for deep-frying

Maple Crème Fraîche

½ cup (125 mL) heavy (35%) cream

½ cup (125 mL) Farmhouse Crème Fraîche (page 225) or store-bought

2 tablespoons (30 mL) pure maple syrup

1 teaspoon (5 mL) pure vanilla extract

butternut squash pie
pumpkin seed crust, bourbon cream

You can easily make a pumpkin pie with a butternut squash instead of a pumpkin because it's all about the spice blend anyway. That is, unless you roast the squash first to concentrate the flavours before gently baking the squash purée in a delicious spiced custard. As homage, ground pumpkin seeds are bound with sugar and butter into a crispy, crunchy crust. Bourbon elevates simple whipped cream to harmonize with the fragrant pumpkin spices.

Make the Pumpkin Seed Crust
Preheat the oven to 350°F (180°C). Turn on the convection fan if you have one.

Measure the pumpkin seeds, white sugar, butter, and salt into a food processor. Grind into coarse crumbs, forming an even dough. Transfer the mixture to a 9 or 10-inch (23 or 25 cm) non-stick pie plate and evenly press across the bottom and up the sides. Top with a similar pie plate and press firmly to form an even pie crust. Perforate the crust with a fork 8 times in an even pattern. (The holes keep it from bubbling and shrinking.) Bake until lightly browned and fragrant, 20 minutes or so. Remove from the oven and reserve until needed. Keep the oven on. Wipe out the food processor.

Make the Butternut Squash Filling and Bake
Place the butternut squash halves cut side up on a baking sheet. Brush with melted butter and bake until soft and lightly browned, 1 hour or so. Remove from the oven and rest until cool.

Transfer the baked squash to a food processor and purée until smooth, scraping down the sides once or twice. Add the cream, brown sugar, eggs, cinnamon, ginger, nutmeg, allspice, and cloves. Process until smooth, scraping down the sides once or twice.

Transfer the purée to the pie crust, smoothing the surface evenly. Bake until the filling is firm, 45 minutes or so. Remove from the oven and rest until completely cool.

Make the Bourbon Cream
Combine the cream, sugar, bourbon, and vanilla and whip until thick.

Slice the cooled pie and serve with generous dollops of whipped bourbon cream and a scattering of thinly sliced squash blossoms.

Makes one 9 or 10-inch (23 or 25 cm) pie, enough for 8 generous slices

Pumpkin Seed Crust

2½ cups (625 mL) raw pumpkin seeds

½ cup (125 mL) white sugar

½ cup (125 mL) butter, melted

Pinch of sea salt

Butternut Squash Filling

1 large butternut squash, peeled, halved lengthwise, and seeds removed

2 tablespoons (30 mL) butter, melted

1½ cups (375 mL) heavy (35%) cream

½ cup (125 mL) firmly packed brown sugar

2 eggs

2 teaspoons (10 mL) cinnamon

1 teaspoon (5 mL) ground ginger

½ teaspoon (2 mL) ground nutmeg

¼ teaspoon (1 mL) ground allspice

¼ teaspoon (1 mL) ground cloves

Bourbon Cream

2 cups (500 mL) heavy (35%) cream

2 tablespoons (30 mL) white sugar

2 tablespoons (30 mL) of your favourite bourbon or other spirit

½ teaspoon (2 mL) pure vanilla extract

3 or 4 squash blossoms, thinly sliced, for garnish

winter squash thyme skillet cake

rosemary vanilla cream

Sweet winter squash chunks are tenderly baked in a rich brown butter batter scented with thyme, the whole served with dollops of whipped cream infused with bold rosemary and harmoniously balanced with extra vanilla. Squashes grown for long-term storage are sweet and deeply delicious, but very tough. As its durable texture softens in this tender cake, its deep flavours emerge. Thyme and rosemary help coax it from the savoury to the sweet kitchen.

Infuse the Rosemary Vanilla Cream

In a small saucepan over low heat, gently warm the cream, white sugar, and rosemary just to a bare simmer, stirring occasionally, until infused with flavour, about 10 minutes. Stir in the vanilla, transfer to a mason jar or other resealable container, and refrigerate overnight.

Make the Winter Squash Thyme Skillet Cake

Toss the butter into a small saucepan over medium-high heat. Swirl gently as it melts, steams, foams, and eventually lightly browns. Remove from the heat, pour into a small bowl, and rest at room temperature until cooled, an hour or so.

Preheat the oven to 350°F (180°C). Turn on the convection fan if you have one. Lightly oil a 10 or 12-inch (25 or 30 cm) cast-iron skillet or heavy non-stick skillet.

In a small bowl, whisk together the flour, baking powder, and salt. Measure the eggs, brown sugar, rum, vanilla, and thyme into the bowl of a stand mixer fitted with the paddle attachment. Beat at high speed until smooth and creamy, 5 minutes or so. Turn off the mixer, pour in the browned butter, then beat until smooth. Turn off the mixer again, add the dry ingredients, and slowly mix until thoroughly, evenly mixed. Remove the bowl from the stand, switch to a wooden spoon, and stir in the squash pieces. Scrape the mixture into the skillet. Vigorously shake and settle the pan contents. Bake until the cake is lightly browned and firm, 60 minutes or so. Remove from the oven and rest until completely cool.

Whip the Rosemary Vanilla Cream

Whip the infused rosemary vanilla cream until thick, a minute or two.

Slice the cooled cake and serve with generous dollops of rosemary vanilla cream, sprinkled with thyme flowers, if using.

Makes one 10 or 12-inch (25 or 30 cm) skillet cake, enough for 8 generous slices

---

Rosemary Vanilla Cream

2 cups (500 mL) heavy (35%) cream

2 tablespoons (30 mL) white sugar

Leaves from 1 sprig of fresh rosemary, very finely minced

1 tablespoon (15 mL) pure vanilla extract

Winter Squash Thyme Skillet Cake

¾ cup (175 mL) butter

1 cup (250 mL) all-purpose flour

1 teaspoon (5 mL) baking powder

½ teaspoon (2 mL) sea salt

3 eggs

1 cup (250 mL) brown sugar

¼ cup (60 mL) dark rum

1 teaspoon (5 mL) pure vanilla extract

Leaves and tender stems from 1 bunch of fresh thyme sprigs, finely minced (2 tablespoons/30 mL or so)

A winter squash of your choice (1 butternut or kabocha squash, 2 or 3 acorn squash, or other winter squash; about 2 pounds/900 g), peeled and cut into 1-inch (2.5 cm) pieces

A handful of fresh thyme flowers (optional), for garnish

farmhouse
pantry

maritime mustard pickles

Chef Craig Flinn began his illustrious culinary career at the Inn at Bay Fortune long before becoming a cookbook author and legendary Nova Scotia chef. His gluten-free mustard pickles are the gold standard for the chutney-style version of this condiment we prefer. All the traditional flavours are included—there's just a bit more cheferly knife work. You'll be rewarded with a bright, distinctive all-purpose condiment and an authentic taste of the Maritimes.

Brine the Vegetables

In a medium pot, bring the water and salt to a full boil. In a medium bowl, stir together the cucumbers, onions, celery, and bell peppers. Pour the boiling salted water over the vegetables. Rest for 2 hours. Drain well.

Pickle and Preserve the Vegetables

In a large pot, stir together the sugar, vinegar, mustard seeds, dry mustard, turmeric, cumin, fenugreek, and chili flakes. Reserve 2 cups (500 mL) of the mixture. Add the drained vegetables to the pot and bring to a full boil over high heat. Reduce to a simmer and cook until tender, flavourful, and reduced, 15 minutes. Meanwhile, stir and dissolve the cornstarch into the reserved vinegar solution, forming a slurry. Return the heat to high, stir in the cornstarch slurry, and cook, stirring constantly, until noticeably thickened, 2 or 3 minutes. Remove from the heat. Pour into mason jars or resealable containers and refrigerate until cool and thickened further, at least 2 hours, even overnight, or for up to several weeks.

Makes 12 cups (3 L)

3 cups (750 mL) water

½ cup (125 mL) kosher salt (we use Windsor)

3 English cucumbers, unpeeled, seeded and finely diced

4 yellow onions, finely diced

2 celery stalks, finely diced

1 green bell pepper, stem and seeds removed, finely diced

1 red bell pepper, stem and seeds removed, finely diced

4 cups (1 L) sugar

3 cups (750 mL) white vinegar

2 tablespoons (30 mL) whole mustard seeds

2 tablespoons (30 mL) dry mustard

2 tablespoons (30 mL) ground turmeric

1 tablespoon (15 mL) ground cumin

1 tablespoon (15 mL) ground fenugreek

1 tablespoon (15 mL) Red Chili Flakes (page 219) or store-bought

½ cup (125 mL) cornstarch

red chili flakes

Makes 1 cup (250 mL)

1 pound (450 g) dried ancho, guajillo, or other medium-heat chili

Our culinary farm tries to produce everything it can for our kitchen, including a reliable source of warm spicy heat. We can't grow peppercorns on Prince Edward Island, but we can do our best to grow chilies. We give the heat-loving plants row-cover greenhouses and lots of attention from our farmers to thrive. We prize medium-heat varietals that balance useful spicy heat with aromatic flavour. Some we brew into fermented hot sauces, others we simply dry and lightly grind into all-purpose coarse flakes. This simple ingredient comes from afar to most kitchens, yet ours comes from Farmer Kevin Petrie and his team's hard work.

Remove the tough woody stems from the dried chilies. Crack the chilies into the bowl of a food processor. Pulse, grinding into coarse flakes. Transfer to a clean jar, tightly seal, and store at room temperature for up to 1 year.

sesame za'atar

Jeff McCourt is a cheesemaker, pizza baker, and wood oven master. His Glasgow Glen Dairy's fire-breathing oven is a Prince Edward Island mecca for its uniquely flavoured wood-fired pizzas crafted with his own cheeses. One of our favourites is sprinkled with the bright flavours of this legendary Middle Eastern spice blend, earthy with tangy undertones and a hint of nuttiness from the sesame seeds. Jeff is always happy to share a jar with a friend.

Measure the thyme, oregano, and cumin seeds into a small skillet. Toss gently over medium heat until lightly toasted and fragrant, 2 minutes or so. Transfer to a spice grinder and cool completely. Add the sumac and salt and coarsely grind. Transfer to small jar and mix in the sesame seeds. Tightly seal and store at room temperature for up to 1 year.

Makes 1 cup (250 mL)

¼ cup (60 mL) dried thyme

¼ cup (60 mL) dried oregano

¼ cup (60 mL) cumin seeds

¼ cup (60 mL) ground sumac

2 tablespoons (30 mL) sea salt

¼ cup (60 mL) toasted sesame seeds

preserved lemon dressing

This bright all-purpose dressing adds just the right balancing finish to many vegetable dishes in our farmhouse kitchen. You can easily fill a jar and keep it in your fridge for regular use.

Measure the ingredients into a 1-cup (250 mL) mason jar. Cover tightly and shake vigorously into a smooth dressing. Alternatively, whisk everything together in a small bowl. Store in a resealable container in the refrigerator for up to 1 week.

Makes about 1 cup (250 mL)

¼ cup (60 mL) Preserved Lemon Purée (page 221)

½ cup (125 mL) extra-virgin olive oil

Zest and juice of 2 lemons

2 tablespoons (30 mL) pure liquid honey

1 tablespoon (15 mL) Dijon mustard

1 teaspoon (5 mL) hot sauce

preserved lemon purée

Our neighbour Louise is legendary for sharing her preserved lemons. They're insanely delicious, so rather than make our own we rely on her to keep us well stocked. For anyone who doesn't live next door, here's her recipe.

6 organic lemons, scrubbed, dried, divided

3 tablespoons (45 mL) coarse sea salt

1 tablespoon (15 mL) coriander seeds

1 bay leaf

Quarter 3 lemons lengthwise, stopping about ½ inch (1 cm) from the bottom so they stay intact. Working with 1 lemon at a time over a small bowl to catch any juices, gently spread open the lemon and remove as many seeds as you can. Sprinkle in 1 tablespoon (15 mL) or so of the salt and some coriander seeds. Close the lemon back up, massaging the salt into the flesh and skin. Repeat with the other 2 quartered lemons. Pack and squish the lemons into a 2-cup (500 mL) mason jar along with the bay leaf and any remaining coriander seeds.

Zest and juice the remaining 3 lemons into the same bowl. Pour into the jar along with any accumulated salt. If the lemons are not submerged in juice, add more until they're covered. Screw the lid on tightly and give the jar a good shake. Refrigerate the lemons for 4 to 6 weeks, shaking and inverting the jar every few days.

After preserving, transfer the lemons and juice to your blender or food processor. Discard the bay leaf and any lemon seeds you come across. Purée until smooth. Use immediately or transfer to a clean jar, tightly seal, and refrigerate for up to 1 year.

lentil sprouts

Makes a few cups

Ounce for ounce, lentil sprouts are one of the most nutrient-dense foods we harvest, and you can easily sprout your own at home.

¼ cup (60 mL) green or brown lentils

Start sprouting the lentils 5 days in advance. Cut a piece of mesh screen about 4 inches (10 cm) square. Pour the lentils into a 4-cup (1 L) mason jar. Cover the jar's mouth with the screen and tighten on the screw ring (don't use the flat lid). This will make it super easy to rinse and drain your sprouts. Fill the jar with water, drain it through the mesh, and fill it again. Soak the lentils for 4 hours or so, then drain well.

Start a twice-daily routine for your lentil babies. Each morning and evening, gently fill the jar with fresh water, rinse the lentils, then drain well through the screen. Try not to let the lentils sit in the water. Rest the jar on its side on a kitchen windowsill. The lentils are starting to grow already, even though you can't see it.

Shortly after the first day, they'll begin to sprout. In just 2 or 3 days, the sprouts will be about ½ inch (1 cm) long, with small green leaves forming on the ends. You can eat them now or save them for later. To save, swap the screen for the jar's lid and refrigerate for up to 1 week.

pickled red onions

Makes 2 cups (500 mL)

This ubiquitous condiment has been a part of the inn's pantry for thirty years. Its sharp tangy flavour and crisp texture balances many of our vegetable salads and sides.

1 cup (250 mL) red wine vinegar

1 cup (250 mL) sugar

1 tablespoon (15 mL) fennel seeds

1 tablespoon (15 mL) coriander seeds

2 bay leaves

2 or 3 red onions, thinly sliced

Measure the red wine vinegar, sugar, fennel seeds, coriander seeds, and bay leaves into a large saucepan. Bring to a full boil over medium-high heat. Gently stir in the red onions. Cover tightly and remove from the heat. Rest at room temperature until cool. Transfer the onions and juices to a 2-cup (500 mL) mason jar, seal, and refrigerate overnight. Store in the refrigerator. The pickled onions are at their best after a few days resting and will last for up to 1 month.

farmhouse chicken broth

Every kitchen needs an all-purpose chicken broth ready to serve as a savoury base for a myriad of meals. For maximum rich flavour we spatchcock the chicken and roast it first before simmering it into broth.

Preheat the oven to 425°F (220°C). Turn on the convection fan if you have one. Preheat a large cast-iron skillet or roasting pan.

Lay the chicken breast side down. With a pair of sharp kitchen shears, cut along each side of the backbone, removing it and the attached neck. Turn the bird over and firmly press down on the breastbone and legs, flattening the bird as best you can. Season generously with salt and pepper.

Carefully place the chicken, skin side up, in the preheated pan. In a medium bowl, toss together the onions, carrots, and celery. Nestle half of the vegetable mixture around the bird, along with the garlic cloves, filling the pan. Roast for 30 minutes. Firmly swirl and shake the pan, evenly coating the vegetables with flavourful juices. Continue roasting until the chicken is crispy, golden brown, and fragrant, another hour or so.

Remove the chicken from the pan. Carefully pour off as much of the flavourful rendered fat as possible and reserve for another use. With a pair of tongs in each hand, pull, tug, and shred off as much of the roasted meat and skin as you can. Cover the meat tightly and reserve for another use. Transfer the roasted vegetables to a large soup or stock pot. Flip the carcass over, exposing the inside. Pour 1 cup (250 mL) or so of the water into the pan, shaking the works to evenly distribute the juices. Return the pan to the oven and continue cooking until the meaty remnants are browned, about 30 minutes.

Remove the pan from the oven. Carefully transfer the chicken carcass to the pot. Pour 4 cups (1 L) of the water into the pan and stir until every single flavourful browned bit has dissolved. Scrape every last drop into the pot. Pour the remaining 7 cups (1.75 L) water into the pot. Toss in the reserved vegetable mixture, thyme, rosemary, and bay leaves. Cover tightly and bring to a slow, steady simmer. Cook, stirring occasionally, until rich and fragrant, an hour or so. Without uncovering, remove from the heat and let sit for an hour.

Strain the broth through a fine-mesh strainer. Taste and adjust seasoning. Discard the solids. Use immediately or transfer to a resealable container and refrigerate for up to 5 days or freeze for 6 months.

Makes about 12 cups (3 L)

1 large roasting chicken (about 5 pounds/2.25 kg)

1 tablespoon (15 mL) sea salt

Freshly ground pepper

6 large white or yellow onions, chopped

4 large carrots, peeled and thinly sliced

4 celery stalks, thinly sliced

Cloves from 1 head of garlic, crushed

12 cups (3 L) water, divided

12 sprigs of fresh thyme

4 sprigs of fresh rosemary

2 bay leaves

farmhouse yogurt

Yogurt is alive—that's the point. It's teeming with living, breathing beneficial organisms, so making more takes some finesse. For best results, use a digital thermometer or the yogurt settings of an Instant Pot.

Make the Starter Batch

Pour the milk into a small pot over medium heat. Patiently warm it, slowly stirring, until it reaches precisely 190°F (88°C) on a digital thermometer. Pour the hot milk into a 4-cup (1 L) mason jar. Seal tightly. Rest, swirling occasionally, until it reaches precisely 110°F (43°C). Stir in the yogurt. Pour into two 2-cup (500 mL) mason jars. Cover each with a square of paper towel and secure by screwing on the ring band. Rest overnight, undisturbed, at precisely 85°F (29°C). Replace the paper towel with the mason jar lid and refrigerate until cold and firm, 4 to 6 hours. Enjoy immediately or refrigerate for up to 5 days, reserving the last ¼ cup (60 mL) for the next batch.

Subsequent Batches

When you are running low, make a new batch following the same procedure. In a clean mason jar, stir together the new milk and ¼ cup (60 mL) of the previous yogurt. Over time your yogurt's bacterial culture will strengthen as it finds balance with your environment. You'll need less to keep the process going, but every batch will taste better.

Each batch makes 4 cups (1 L)

Starter Batch

4 cups (1 L) whole milk

½ cup (125 mL) natural plain full-fat yogurt or plain Greek yogurt

Each Subsequent Batch

4 cups (1 L) whole milk

¼ cup (60 mL) of the previous batch of yogurt

farmhouse crème fraîche

Sour cream harnesses the natural bacteria in our environment in the name of rich, tangy flavour, thick and delicious texture, and essential gut health.

Make the Starter Batch

Stir together the cream and buttermilk in a 4-cup (1 L) mason jar. Cover with a square of paper towel and secure by screwing on the ring band. Rest, undisturbed, at room temperature until the contents thicken noticeably, 24 hours or more. Enjoy immediately or replace the paper towel with the mason jar lid and refrigerate for up to 5 days, reserving the last ¼ cup (60 mL) for the next batch.

Subsequent Batches

When you're running low, make a new batch following the same procedure. In a clean mason jar, stir together the new cream and ¼ cup (60 mL) of the previous sour cream. Cover with paper towel, secure with the ring band, and rest at room temperature until thickened.

Each batch makes 2 cups (500 mL)

Starter Batch
2 cups (500 mL) heavy (35%) cream

¼ cup (60 mL) buttermilk

Each Subsequent Batch
2 cups (500 mL) heavy (35%) cream

¼ cup (60 mL) of the previous batch of crème fraiche

fresh ricotta with rosemary

There are many ways to make cheese, but this one is possibly the simplest. The woodsy fragrance of rosemary is particularly well suited to homemade ricotta.

Measure the milk, cream, rosemary (if using), and salt into a large saucepan. Gently heat over medium heat to 190°F (88°C), using a digital thermometer for accuracy, stirring frequently to prevent scorching. Remove from the heat and briefly stir in the lemon juice. Rest, undisturbed, as curds and whey form, 30 minutes.

Line a fine-mesh strainer with several layers of cheesecloth and place it over a large bowl. Pour the milk mixture through the lined strainer and let drain for 1 hour. Cover with plastic wrap, transfer to the refrigerator, and let strain overnight. Reserve the whey for another use. Use the cheese immediately or transfer to a resealable container and refrigerate for up to 3 days.

Makes about 2 cups (500 mL)

4 cups (1 L) whole milk

1 cup (250 mL) heavy (35%) cream

Leaves from 2 sprigs of fresh rosemary, finely minced (optional)

½ teaspoon (2 mL) sea salt

2 tablespoons (30 mL) lemon juice

farmhouse crème fraîche

Sour cream harnesses the natural bacteria in our environment in the name of rich, tangy flavour, thick and delicious texture, and essential gut health.

Make the Starter Batch
Stir together the cream and buttermilk in a 4-cup (1 L) mason jar. Cover with a square of paper towel and secure by screwing on the ring band. Rest, undisturbed, at room temperature until the contents thicken noticeably, 24 hours or more. Enjoy immediately or replace the paper towel with the mason jar lid and refrigerate for up to 5 days, reserving the last ¼ cup (60 mL) for the next batch.

Subsequent Batches
When you're running low, make a new batch following the same procedure. In a clean mason jar, stir together the new cream and ¼ cup (60 mL) of the previous sour cream. Cover with paper towel, secure with the ring band, and rest at room temperature until thickened.

Each batch makes 2 cups (500 mL)

Starter Batch
2 cups (500 mL) heavy (35%) cream

¼ cup (60 mL) buttermilk

Each Subsequent Batch
2 cups (500 mL) heavy (35%) cream

¼ cup (60 mL) of the previous batch of crème fraiche

fresh ricotta with rosemary

There are many ways to make cheese, but this one is possibly the simplest. The woodsy fragrance of rosemary is particularly well suited to homemade ricotta.

Measure the milk, cream, rosemary (if using), and salt into a large saucepan. Gently heat over medium heat to 190°F (88°C), using a digital thermometer for accuracy, stirring frequently to prevent scorching. Remove from the heat and briefly stir in the lemon juice. Rest, undisturbed, as curds and whey form, 30 minutes.

Line a fine-mesh strainer with several layers of cheesecloth and place it over a large bowl. Pour the milk mixture through the lined strainer and let drain for 1 hour. Cover with plastic wrap, transfer to the refrigerator, and let strain overnight. Reserve the whey for another use. Use the cheese immediately or transfer to a resealable container and refrigerate for up to 3 days.

Makes about 2 cups (500 mL)

4 cups (1 L) whole milk

1 cup (250 mL) heavy (35%) cream

Leaves from 2 sprigs of fresh rosemary, finely minced (optional)

½ teaspoon (2 mL) sea salt

2 tablespoons (30 mL) lemon juice

special ingredients, farm resources, and contacts

Many of the recipes in this book call for a specific ingredient from a particular supplier. In most cases a substitution is noted. If you're striving for authenticity, you can contact the supplier directly. Our culinary farm relies on these trusted suppliers.

Cold-Pressed Organic Canola Oil

Alpha Mills
Heatherdale, Prince Edward Island
alphamillsinc.com

Cheese

Avonlea Clothbound Cheddar
Cows Creamery
Charlottetown, Prince Edward Island
cowscreamery.ca

Glasgow Glen Farm Gouda Cheese
Glasgow Glen Farm
New Glasgow, Prince Edward Island
glasgowglenfarm.ca

Fresh Salmon

Sustainable Blue
Centre Burlington, Nova Scotia
sustainableblue.com

Cold-Smoked Salmon

Oven Head Salmon Smokers
Bethel, New Brunswick
ovenheadsmokers.com

Bottled Bar Clams

Annand Clams
Ellerslie, Prince Edward Island
annands.com

Afishionado
Bedford, Nova Scotia
afishionado.ca

Honey

Island Gold Honey
Montague, Prince Edward Island
islandgoldhoney.ca

Microgreens

Bramble Hill Farm
Wolfville, Nova Scotia
bramblehill.ca

Artisanal Hard Cider

Double Hill Cidery
Caledonia, Prince Edward Island
doublehill.ca

Cider Vinegar

Boates Farm
Woodville, Nova Scotia
boatesfarm.ca

Legal Moonshine

Myriad View Artisan Distillery
Rollo Bay, Prince Edward Island
straitshine.com

Generic Seeds

Veseys Seeds
York, Prince Edward Island
veseys.com

West Coast Seeds
Ladner, British Columbia
westcoastseeds.com

Specialty Seeds

Johnny's Selected Seeds
Winslow, Maine, USA
johnnyseeds.com

Heirloom Seeds

Baker Creek Heirloom Seeds
Mansfield, Missouri, USA
rareseeds.com

Specialized Farm Tools

Dubois Agrinovation
Saint-Rémi, Quebec
duboisag.com

my special thanks

To Farmer Kevin Petrie for sharing my vision for a culinary farm and leading its development through your deeply personal embrace of sustainable, regenerative agriculture. I am honoured to be on your team.

To Nghe and Al for your incredible creative collaboration and the wonderful imagery it gave us. To Chris for your invaluable insight. To time together crafting our best flavours.

To Rene, the gigantic gentleman of our farm who lovingly escorts our harvest to the kitchen, to Stephanie for your bright leadership, to Mike for your humble enthusiasm, and to Adriana for your quiet intensity.

To our chefs' brigade for enthusiastically supporting our mission, embracing our farm, working our soil, and sharing our collective harvest with our guests.

To our guests and my readers who so graciously share time with us, allowing our collective growth to continue. We are so very thankful for the opportunity.

To Vanessa, Jennifer, and our entire team, we are all so fortunate!

Most especially to my family, Gabe, Ariella, Camille, and my favourite farmer, my wife Chastity, and our many harvests together.

index

A

Almond Butter, Carrot, 106
ancho chilies
    Ancho Squeeze, 93
    Kabocha Squash and Ancho
        Cider Broth, 51–53
    Red Chili Flakes, 219
    Whole Roasted Cauliflower, 136
anchovy fillets
    Fennel Frond Dressing, 168
    Tarragon Tonnato, 151
anise liqueur: Fennel Marmalade,
    124
"Anne's Mistake" Raspberry
    Cordial, 198
apples/apple cider
    Cider-Braised Baby Leeks and
        Warm Apple Vinaigrette, 98
    Cranberry Rosemary Chutney, 79
    Kabocha Squash and Ancho
        Cider Broth, 51–53
    Pan-Roasted Cauliflower, Leek,
        Apple, and Cinnamon-
        Crusted Pork Tenderloin, 189
    Slow-Roasted Duck and Winter
        Vegetables, 186
    Whole Roasted Cauliflower, 136
Arugula Dill Salad, 175–176
Asparagus Dill Frittata, 57

B

Baba Ganoush, Grilled Eggplant,
    123
bacon see also pork
    Bacon, Baked Beans, and Kale,
        164
    Bacon-Steamed Baby Turnips and
        Greens, 155
Baked Potatoes and Cracklings, 163
Baked Tomatoes, Fennel, Garlic,
    and Feta, 54
basil, fresh
    Basil Ratatouille and Swiss Chard
        Wraps, 117–118
    Grilled Corn Basil Relish, 159
    Quinoa Feta Stuffed Bell Peppers,
        60
    Soba Noodle Bowl, 63

beans
    Bacon, Baked Beans, and Kale,
        164
    Baked Tomatoes, Fennel, Garlic,
        and Feta, 54
    Bok Choy and Edamame, 64
    Grilled Summer Salad, 171
    Mushy Green Beans and
        Tarragon, 106
    Sorrel Hummus, 33
    Spicy Roasted Chickpeas, 51–53
Béarnaise Sauce, Brown Butter, 119
beef
    Beefy Roast Potatoes, 163
    Beefy Vegetable Stew, 177–178
    Farmhouse Beef Broth, 177–178
    Grilled Summer Salad, 171
    Potatoes and Beef, 163
beets
    Beets, Fire Grains, and Fresh
        Ricotta with Rosemary, 45–46
    Roasted Beets, 80
    Rosemary Beet Purée, 70–72
bell peppers
    Basil Ratatouille, 117–118
    Grilled Corn Basil Relish, 159
    Quinoa Feta Stuffed Bell Peppers,
        60
blueberries: Tarragon Blueberry
    Stew, 211
Bok Choy and Edamame, 64
borage flowers: Garden Tangle, 38
Bourbon Cream, 212
bowls
    Bok Choy and Edamame, 64
    Shiitake Gai Lan Noodle Bowl, 37
    Soba Noodle Bowl with
        Golden Tofu, Garden Peas,
        Cinnamon Basil, and Miso
        Carrot Broth, 63
Brandade, Smoked Salmon Celery
    Root, 156
broccoli
    Broccoli Clam Chowder, 160
    Broccoli Garlic Sauce, 131
broccoli sprouts: Roasted Brussels
    Sprouts, Bean Sprouts, Broccoli
    Sprouts, and Cashews, 135

Broccolini, Grilled, 132
broths see also soups and stews
    Farmhouse Beef Broth, 177–178
    Farmhouse Chicken Broth, 223
    Ginger Lime Coconut Broth, 64
    Kabocha Squash and Ancho
        Cider Broth, 51–53
    Melted Cabbage, Turnip, and
        Ham Hock, 185
    Miso Carrot Broth, 63
    Vegetable Broth, 34
Brown Butter Béarnaise Sauce, 119
Brussels Sprouts, Roasted, Bean
    Sprouts, Broccoli Sprouts, and
    Cashews, 135
burnet leaves: Garden Tangle, 38
butter
    Brown Butter Béarnaise Sauce,
        119
    Carrot Almond Butter, 106
    Herb Butter, 75
    Rosemary Maple Brown Butter,
        87
    Spiced Brown Butter Hollandaise,
        136
butternut squash
    Butternut Squash Pie, 212
    Roasted Butternut Squash Steaks,
        143

C

cabbage
    Melted Cabbage, Turnip, and
        Ham Hock, 185
    Shiitake Cabbage Tacos, 43–44
    Vietnamese Slaw, 152
    Wilted Cabbage, 140
Cake, Winter Squash Thyme Skillet,
    215
capers: Tarragon Tonnato, 151
caraway seeds
    Caraway Rye Crackers, 156
    Caraway Rye Crust, 59
carrots
    Beefy Vegetable Stew, 177–178
    Carrot Almond Butter, 106
    Carrot Cake Cookies, 201–202
    Carrot Horseradish Jam, 83

Farmhouse Beef Broth, 177–178
Farmhouse Chicken Broth, 223
Grilled Carrots, 83
Lentil Soup, 49–50
Miso Carrot Broth, 63
Root Vegetable and Roast
   Chicken Pan Stew, 182
Root Vegetable Chowder, 75
Root Vegetable Pavé, 70–72
Vegetable Broth, 34
Vietnamese Slaw, 152
cashews
   Cilantro Cashew Pesto, 144
   Roasted Brussels Sprouts, Bean
      Sprouts, Broccoli Sprouts,
      and Cashews, 135
cauliflower
   Cauliflower Chickpea Fritters, 131
   Cauliflower Cream, 139
   Cauliflower Mac 'n' Cheese, 59
   Cauliflower Steaks, 139
   Pan-Roasted Cauliflower, Leek,
      Apple, and Cinnamon-
      Crusted Pork Tenderloin, 189
   Whole Roasted Cauliflower, 136
celery
   Celery Lovage Slaw, 76
   Farmhouse Beef Broth, 177–178
   Farmhouse Chicken Broth, 223
   Vegetable Broth, 34
celery root
   Celery Lovage Slaw, 76
   Root Vegetable and Roast
      Chicken Pan Stew, 182
   Root Vegetable Chowder, 75
   Root Vegetable Pavé, 70–72
   Smoked Salmon Celery Root
      Brandade, 156
   Whole Roasted Celery Root, 76
cheese
   Baked Tomatoes, Fennel, Garlic,
      and Feta, 54
   Cauliflower Mac 'n' Cheese, 59
   Cilantro Cashew Pesto, 144
   Fresh Ricotta with Rosemary, 225
   Quinoa Feta Stuffed Bell Peppers,
      60
   Sage, Pumpkin Seed, and Goat
      Cheese Pesto, 51–53
   Tomatoes, Nasturtiums, and
      Golden Halloumi, 41
chicken
   Chef Nghe Tran's Goi Ga, 152
   Farmhouse Chicken Broth, 223
   Potato, Leek, Mushroom, and
      Chicken Skillet Stew, 167

Root Vegetable and Roast
   Chicken Pan Stew, 182
chickpea flour
   Cauliflower Chickpea Fritters, 131
   Cumin Corn Fritters, 93–94
   Pea and Mint Fritters, 49–50
chickpeas
   Baked Tomatoes, Fennel, Garlic,
      and Feta, 54
   Sorrel Hummus, 33
   Spicy Roasted Chickpeas, 51–53
chilies
   Ancho Squeeze, 93
   Kabocha Squash and Ancho
      Cider Broth, 51–53
   Nuoc Cham, 152
   Red Chili Flakes, 219
   Sumac Chili Oil, 33
   Whole Roasted Cauliflower, 136
Chimichurri, Parsley, 84
Chips, Za'atar-Spiced Eggplant, 123
chives, fresh
   Potato Turnip Mash, 87
   Whole Roasted Onions, Grilled
      Garlic Scapes, and Chive
      Flowers, 101–102
Chocolate Chip Cookies, Jalapeño,
   207
chowders
   Broccoli Clam, 160
   Corn and Smoked Salmon, 159
   Root Vegetable, 75
Chutney, Cranberry Rosemary, 79
Cider-Braised Baby Leeks, 98
cilantro
   Cilantro Cashew Pesto, 144
   Green Coriander Seed Salsa, 113
cinnamon basil, fresh: Soba Noodle
   Bowl with Golden Tofu, Garden
   Peas, Cinnamon Basil, and Miso
   Carrot Broth, 63
Cinnamon-Crusted Pork Tenderloin,
   189
Clam Chowder, Broccoli, 160
cocktails
   "Anne's Mistake" Raspberry
      Cordial, 198
   Herb House Lemonade, 194
   Tomato Lillet Splash, 193
coconut/coconut milk
   Ginger Lime Coconut Broth, 64
   Lentil Soup, 49–50
Compote, Strawberry Rhubarb,
   203–204
condiments see also dips; sauces
   Carrot Horseradish Jam, 83

Cranberry Rosemary Chutney, 79
Fennel Marmalade, 124
Green Jam, 43
Grilled Corn Basil Relish, 159
Grilled Corn Poblano Relish, 114
Mushroom Ketchup, 97
Tomato Garlic Mash, 181
Confit Tomato, Poblano, and Garlic,
   110
cookies
   Carrot Cake, 201–202
   Jalapeño Chocolate Chip, 207
Cordial, "Anne's Mistake"
   Raspberry, 198
coriander seeds
   Green Coriander Seed Salsa, 113
   Green Jam, 43
corn
   Corn and Smoked Salmon
      Chowder, 159
   Cumin Corn Fritters, 93–94
   Grilled Corn Basil Relish, 159
   Grilled Corn Poblano Relish, 114
   Sweet Corn Fritters, 211
Cracked Potatoes, 88
crackers
   Caraway Rye, 156
   Sourdough, 33
Cranberry Rosemary Chutney, 79
creams
   Bourbon Cream, 212
   Farmhouse Crème Fraîche, 225
   Lavender Cream, 203–204
   Maple Crème Fraîche, 211
   Rosemary Vanilla Cream, 215
cremini mushrooms: Mushroom
   Ketchup, 97
Crispy Leeks, 98
Crispy Onions, 106
Crispy Shallots, 101
crusts
   Caraway Rye, 59
   Pumpkin Seed, 212
cucumbers, English
   Cucumber Gin Ice Pops, 197
   Cucumber Radish Salad with
      Tarragon Tonnato, 151
   Green Coriander Seed Salsa, 113
   Maritime Mustard Pickles, 218
   Radish, Smashed Cucumber, Tofu,
      and Hemp Heart Salad, 38
cumin seeds
   Cumin Browned Onions, 67
   Cumin Corn Fritters, Fresh Pea
      Mash, and Purslane, 93–94
   Sesame Za'atar, 220

D

desserts
Butternut Squash Pie, 212
Carrot Cake Cookies, 201–202
Cucumber Gin Ice Pops, 197
Ice Cream Sandwiches, 201–202
Jalapeño Chocolate Chip
Cookies, 207
Old-School Rhubarb, 208
Strawberry Rhubarb Pavlova,
203–204
Sweet Corn Fritters, 211
Winter Squash Thyme Skillet
Cake, 215
dill, fresh
Arugula Dill Salad, 175–176
Asparagus Dill Frittata, 57
Smoked Salmon Celery Root
Brandade, 156
dips see also condiments
Grilled Eggplant Baba Ganoush,
123
Sage, Pumpkin Seed, and Goat
Cheese Pesto, 51–53
Smoked Salmon Celery Root
Brandade, 156
Sorrel Hummus, 33
dressings see also sauces
Farmhouse, 109
Fennel Frond, 168
Honey, 41
Kimchi Miso, 135
Lemon Garlic Yogurt, 171
Preserved Lemon, 220
drinks
"Anne's Mistake" Raspberry
Cordial, 198
Herb House Lemonade, 194
Tomato Lillet Splash, 193
Vegetable Tea, 34
Duck, Slow-Roasted, and Winter
Vegetables, 186

E

Edamame, Bok Choy and, 64
eggplants
Basil Ratatouille, 117–118
Grilled Eggplant Baba Ganoush,
123
Roast Eggplant-Wrapped Salmon,
181
Za'atar-Spiced Eggplant Chips, 123
eggs
Asparagus Dill Frittata, 57
Brown Butter Béarnaise Sauce, 119
Parsnip Ice Cream, 201–202

Potato-Crusted Smoked Salmon
Cakes, 175–176
Spiced Brown Butter Hollandaise,
136
Strawberry Rhubarb Pavlova,
203–204
enoki mushrooms
Enoki Nori Tarragon Tangle, 37
Shiitake Cabbage Tacos, 43–44

F

Farmhouse Beef Broth, 177–178
Farmhouse Chicken Broth, 223
Farmhouse Crème Fraîche, 225
Farmhouse Dressing, 109
Farmhouse Yogurt, 224
fennel
Baked Tomatoes, Fennel, Garlic,
and Feta, 54
Fennel Frond Dressing, 168
Fennel Marmalade, 124
Fennel Mustard Pickle Slaw, 127
Slow-Roasted Pork, Poblano,
Fennel, and Tomatoes, 168
Vegetable Broth, 34
feta cheese
Baked Tomatoes, Fennel, Garlic,
and Feta, 54
Quinoa Feta Stuffed Bell Peppers,
60
Fire Grains, 45
fish and seafood
Broccoli Clam Chowder, 160
Corn and Smoked Salmon
Chowder, 159
Cucumber Radish Salad with
Tarragon Tonnato, 151
Potato-Crusted Smoked Salmon
Cakes, 175–176
Roast Eggplant-Wrapped Salmon,
181
Smoked Salmon Celery Root
Brandade, 156
fish sauce: Nuoc Cham, 152
Flowers, Greens, Herbs, and, 109
freekeh: Beets, Fire Grains, and
Fresh Ricotta with Rosemary,
45–46
Fresh Ice Plant Salsa, 128
Fresh Pea Mash and Purslane,
93–94
Fresh Ricotta with Rosemary, 225
Fried Sunchokes, 97
Frittata, Asparagus Dill, 57
fritters
Cauliflower Chickpea, 131

Cumin Corn, 93–94
Pea and Mint, 49–50
Sweet Corn, 211

G

gai lan: Shiitake Gai Lan Noodle
Bowl, 37
Garden Tangle, 38
garlic
Baked Tomatoes, Fennel,
Garlic, and Feta, 54
Broccoli Clam Chowder, 160
Broccoli Garlic Sauce, 131
Confit Tomato, Poblano,
and Garlic, 110
Farmhouse Beef Broth,
177–178
Grilled Broccolini, 132
Lemon Garlic Yogurt Dressing,
171
Lentil Soup, 49–50
Parsley Chimichurri, 84
Quinoa Feta Stuffed Bell Peppers,
60
Roast Garlic Labneh, 70–71
Smoked Salmon Celery Root
Brandade, 156
Tomato Garlic Mash, 181
Vegetable Broth, 34
Whole Roasted Onions, Grilled
Garlic Scapes, and Chive
Flowers, 101–102
garnishes
Crispy Leeks, 98
Crispy Onions, 106
Crispy Shallots, 101
Enoki Nori Tarragon Tangle, 37
Garden Tangle, 38
Lovage Oil, 76
Salad Tangle, 91–92
Spicy Roasted Chickpeas, 51–53
Sumac Chili Oil, 33
gin
"Anne's Mistake" Raspberry
Cordial, 198
Cucumber Gin Ice Pops, 197
ginger
Ginger Lime Coconut Broth, 64
Miso Carrot Broth, 63
Nuoc Cham, 152
Gnocchi, Potato, 91–92
goat cheese
Asparagus Dill Frittata, 57
Sage, Pumpkin Seed, and Goat
Cheese Pesto, 51–53, 143
Golden Tofu, 63

grains
  Beets, Fire Grains, and Fresh
    Ricotta with Rosemary, 45–46
  Quinoa Feta Stuffed Bell Peppers,
    60
green beans
  Grilled Summer Salad, 171
  Mushy Green Beans and
    Tarragon, 106
Green Coriander Seed Salsa, 113
Green Jam, 43
Green Lentil Smear, 43–44
Greens, Herbs, and Flowers, 109
Grilled Broccolini, 132
Grilled Carrots, 83
Grilled Corn Basil Relish, 159
Grilled Corn Poblano Relish, 114
Grilled Eggplant Baba Ganoush,
  123
Grilled Parsnips, 84
Grilled Summer Salad, 171
Grilled Summer Squash, 114
Grilled Zucchini, 113

H
halloumi cheese: Tomatoes,
  Nasturtiums, and Golden
  Halloumi, 41
ham: Melted Cabbage, Turnip,
  and Ham Hock, 185
hemp hearts: Radish, Smashed
  Cucumber, Tofu, and Hemp
  Heart Salad, 38
Herb Butter, 75
Herb House Lemonade, 194
Herbs, Greens, and Flowers, 109
Hollandaise, Spiced Brown Butter,
  136
honey
  Carrot Horseradish Jam, 83
  Farmhouse Dressing, 109
  Honey Dressing, 41
  Honey-Roasted Sunflower
    Head, 147
horseradish
  Carrot Horseradish Jam, 83
  Cauliflower Cream, 139
Hummus, Sorrel, 33

I
Ice Cream, Parsnip, 201–202
Ice Cream Sandwiches,
  201–202
Ice Plant Salsa, Fresh, 128
Ice Pops, Cucumber Gin, 197

J
jalapeño peppers
  Green Coriander Seed Salsa,
    113
  Green Jam, 43
  Jalapeño Chocolate Chip
    Cookies, 207
  Tomato Marigold Salsa, 117–118
jams
  Carrot Horseradish, 83
  Green, 43

K
Kabocha Squash and Ancho Cider
  Broth, 51–53
Kalamata olives
  Baked Tomatoes, Fennel, Garlic,
    and Feta, 54
  Quinoa Feta Stuffed Bell Peppers,
    60
kale
  Bacon, Baked Beans, and Kale,
    164
  Mujadara and Wilted Kale, 67
Ketchup, Mushroom, 97
Kimchi Miso Dressing, 135
king mushrooms: Potato, Leek,
  Mushroom, and Chicken Skillet
  Stew, 167

L
labneh
  Mint, 80
  Roast Garlic, 70–71
Lavender Cream, 203–204
leeks
  Cider-Braised Baby Leeks and
    Warm Apple Vinaigrette, 98
  Crispy Leeks, 98
  Pan-Roasted Cauliflower, Leek,
    Apple, and Cinnamon-
    Crusted Pork Tenderloin, 189
  Potato, Leek, Mushroom, and
    Chicken Skillet Stew, 167
lemons
  "Anne's Mistake" Raspberry
    Cordial, 198
  Chef Nghe Tran's Goi Ga, 152
  Herb House Lemonade, 194
  Honey Dressing, 41
  Lemon Garlic Yogurt Dressing, 171
  Nuoc Cham, 152
  Preserved Lemon Dressing, 220
  Preserved Lemon Purée, 221
  Smoked Salmon Celery Root
    Brandade, 156

lentils
  Green Lentil Smear, 43–44
  Lentil Soup, 49–50
  Lentil Sprouts, 222
  Mujadara and Wilted Kale, 67
lettuces: Greens, Herbs, and
  Flowers, 109
Lillet Splash, Tomato, 193
limes
  Ancho Squeeze, 93
  Fresh Ice Plant Salsa, 128
  Ginger Lime Coconut Broth, 64
  Grilled Corn Basil Relish, 159
Lion's Mane Mushroom Steaks,
  119–120
lovage leaves
  Celery Lovage Slaw, 76
  Lovage Oil, 76

M
Mac 'n' Cheese, Cauliflower, 59
Many Peas and Mint Salad, 105
maple syrup
  Bacon, Baked Beans, and Kale,
    164
  Maple Crème Fraîche, 211
  Maple-Spiced Sweet Potato, 144
  Rosemary Maple Brown Butter,
    87
  Tarragon Blueberry Stew, 211
marigold flowers/leaves
  Marigold Ice Cubes, 193
  Tomato Marigold Salsa, 117–118
Maritime Mustard Pickles, 218
Marmalade, Fennel, 124
mayonnaise
  Celery Lovage Slaw, 76
  Tarragon Tonnato, 151
meat dishes
  Bacon, Baked Beans, and Kale,
    164
  Bacon-Steamed Baby Turnips and
    Greens, 155
  Beefy Vegetable Stew, 177–178
  Melted Cabbage, Turnip, and
    Ham Hock, 185
  Pan-Roasted Cauliflower, Leek,
    Apple, and Cinnamon-
    Crusted Pork Tenderloin, 189
  Potato, Leek, Mushroom, and
    Chicken Skillet Stew, 167
  Potatoes and Beef, 163
  Root Vegetable and Roast
    Chicken Pan Stew, 182
  Slow-Roasted Duck and Winter
    Vegetables, 186

Slow-Roasted Pork, Poblano,
Fennel, and Tomatoes,
168
Melted Cabbage, Turnip, and
Ham Hock, 185
meringue: Strawberry Rhubarb
Pavlova, 203–204
mint, fresh
Many Peas and Mint Salad,
105
Mint Labneh, 80
Minted Pea Purée, 105
Pea and Mint Fritters, 49–50
Vietnamese Slaw, 152
miso, yellow
Carrot Almond Butter, 106
Kimchi Miso Dressing, 135
Miso Carrot Broth, 63
Miso Turnip Purée, 171
Mujadara and Wilted Kale, 67
mung bean sprouts
Grilled Summer Salad, 171
Roasted Brussels Sprouts, Bean
Sprouts, Broccoli Sprouts,
and Cashews, 135
mushrooms
Enoki Nori Tarragon Tangle, 37
Lion's Mane Mushroom Steaks,
119–120
Mushroom Ketchup, 97
Potato, Leek, Mushroom, and
Chicken Skillet Stew, 167
Shiitake Cabbage Tacos, 43–44
Shiitake Gai Lan Noodle Bowl,
37
Vegetable Broth, 34
Mushy Green Beans and Tarragon,
106
Mustard Pickles, Maritime, 218

N

nasturtium flowers/leaves:
Tomatoes, Nasturtiums, and
Golden Halloumi, 41
noodles *see also* pastas
Shiitake Gai Lan Noodle Bowl, 37
Soba Noodle Bowl with
Golden Tofu, Garden Peas,
Cinnamon Basil, and Miso
Carrot Broth, 63
nori: Enoki Nori Tarragon Tangle, 37
Nuoc Cham, 152
nutmeg
Nutmeg Soubise, 101–102
Nutmeg Spinach Sauce, 91
nuts *see* almond butter; cashews

O

oats: Carrot Cake Cookies, 201–202
oils
Lovage, 76
Sumac Chili, 33
Old-School Rhubarb, 208
olives, Kalamata
Baked Tomatoes, Fennel, Garlic,
and Feta, 54
Quinoa Feta Stuffed Bell Peppers,
60
onions
Crispy Onions, 106
Cumin Browned Onions, 67
Nutmeg Soubise, 101–102
Pickled Red Onions, 222
Whole Roasted Onions, Grilled
Garlic Scapes, and Chive
Flowers, 101–102
orach leaves: Potato Gnocchi,
Nutmeg Spinach Sauce, and
Orach Salad, 91–92
oyster sauce: Grilled Broccolini, 132

P

Pan-Roasted Cauliflower, Leek,
Apple, and Cinnamon-Crusted
Pork Tenderloin, 189
pantry essentials
Farmhouse Chicken Broth, 223
Farmhouse Crème Fraîche, 225
Farmhouse Yogurt, 224
Fresh Ricotta with Rosemary, 225
Lentil Sprouts, 222
Maritime Mustard Pickles, 218
Pickled Red Onions, 222
Preserved Lemon Dressing, 220
Preserved Lemon Purée, 221
Red Chili Flakes, 219
Sesame Za'atar, 220
Parmigiano-Reggiano cheese:
Cilantro Cashew Pesto, 144
Parsley Chimichurri, 84
parsnips
Beefy Vegetable Stew, 177–178
Grilled Parsnips, 84
Parsnip Ice Cream, 201–202
Root Vegetable and Roast
Chicken Pan Stew, 182
Root Vegetable Chowder, 75
Root Vegetable Pavé, 70–72
Vegetable Broth, 34
pastas *see also* noodles
Baked Tomatoes, Fennel, Garlic,
and Feta, 54
Cauliflower Mac 'n' Cheese, 59

Potato Gnocchi, Nutmeg Spinach
Sauce, and Orach Salad,
91–92
Pavé, Root Vegetable, 70–72
Pavlova, Strawberry Rhubarb,
203–204
peas
Fresh Pea Mash and Purslane,
93–94
Many Peas and Mint Salad, 105
Minted Pea Purée, 105
Pea and Mint Fritters, 49–50
Soba Noodle Bowl with
Golden Tofu, Garden Peas,
Cinnamon Basil, and Miso
Carrot Broth, 63
peppers *see* bell peppers; chilies;
jalapeño peppers; poblano
peppers
pestos
Cilantro Cashew, 144
Sage, Pumpkin Seed, and Goat
Cheese, 51–53, 143
pickles
Maritime Mustard Pickles, 218
Pickled Red Onions, 222
Pie, Butternut Squash, 212
poblano peppers
Confit Tomato, Poblano, and
Garlic, 110
Fresh Ice Plant Salsa, 128
Grilled Corn Basil Relish, 159
Grilled Corn Poblano Relish, 114
Quinoa Feta Stuffed Bell Peppers,
60
Slow-Roasted Pork, Poblano,
Fennel, and Tomatoes, 168
pork *see also* bacon
Cinnamon-Crusted Pork
Tenderloin, 189
Melted Cabbage, Turnip, and
Ham Hock, 185
Slow-Roasted Pork, Poblano,
Fennel, and Tomatoes, 168
potatoes
Beefy Roast Potatoes, 163
Beefy Vegetable Stew, 177–178
Cracked Potatoes, 88
Potato, Leek, Mushroom, and
Chicken Skillet Stew, 167
Potato Gnocchi, Nutmeg Spinach
Sauce, and Orach Salad,
91–92
Potato Turnip Mash, 87
Potato-Crusted Smoked Salmon
Cakes, 175–176

Potatoes and Beef, 163
Root Vegetable and Roast
    Chicken Pan Stew, 182
Root Vegetable Chowder, 75
Root Vegetable Pavé, 70–72
potatoes, sweet
    Maple-Spiced Sweet Potato, 144
    Root Vegetable Pavé, 70–72
    Sweet Potato Jasmine Rice, 64
Preserved Lemon Dressing, 220
Preserved Lemon Purée, 221
pumpkin seeds
    Pumpkin Seed Crust, 212
    Sage, Pumpkin Seed, and Goat
        Cheese Pesto, 51–53, 143
purées
    Minted Pea, 105
    Miso Turnip, 171
    Preserved Lemon, 221
    Rosemary Beet, 70–72
Purslane, Fresh Pea Mash and, 93–94

Q
Quinoa Feta Stuffed Bell Peppers,
    60

R
radishes
    Cucumber Radish Salad, 151
    Radish, Smashed Cucumber, Tofu,
        and Hemp Heart Salad, 38
raisins, dark
    Carrot Cake Cookies, 201–202
    Mujadara and Wilted Kale, 67
Raspberry Cordial, "Anne's
    Mistake", 198
Ratatouille, Basil, and Swiss Chard
    Wraps, 117–118
Raw, Roasted, and Puréed Beets,
    45–46
Red Chili Flakes, 219
relishes
    Grilled Corn Basil, 159
    Grilled Corn Poblano, 114
rhubarb
    Old-School Rhubarb, 208
    Strawberry Rhubarb Compote,
        203–204
    Strawberry Rhubarb Pavlova,
        203–204
rice
    Mujadara and Wilted Kale, 67
    Sweet Potato Jasmine Rice, 64
Ricotta, Fresh, with Rosemary, 225
Roast Eggplant-Wrapped Salmon,
    181

Roast Garlic Labneh, 70–71
Roasted Beets, 80
Roasted Brussels Sprouts, Bean
    Sprouts, Broccoli Sprouts,
    and Cashews, 135
Roasted Butternut Squash Steaks,
    143
Root Vegetable and Roast Chicken
    Pan Stew, 182
Root Vegetable Chowder, 75
Root Vegetable Pavé, 70–72
rosemary, fresh
    Cranberry Rosemary Chutney, 79
    Farmhouse Chicken Broth, 223
    Fresh Ricotta with Rosemary, 225
    Rosemary Beet Purée, 70–72
    Rosemary Maple Brown Butter,
        87
    Rosemary Vanilla Cream, 215
rye bread/flour
    Caraway Rye Crackers, 156
    Caraway Rye Crust, 59

S
sage, fresh
    Cracked Potatoes, 88
    Sage, Pumpkin Seed, and Goat
        Cheese Pesto, 51–53, 143
salads see also slaws
    Arugula Dill Salad, 175–176
    Cucumber Radish Salad, 151
    Greens, Herbs, and Flowers, 109
    Grilled Summer Salad, 171
    Many Peas and Mint Salad, 105
    Radish, Smashed Cucumber, Tofu,
        and Hemp Heart Salad, 38
    Shaved Asparagus Salad, 57
    Tomatoes, Nasturtiums, and
        Golden Halloumi, 41
salmon
    Corn and Smoked Salmon
        Chowder, 159
    Potato-Crusted Smoked Salmon
        Cakes, 175–176
    Roast Eggplant-Wrapped Salmon,
        181
    Smoked Salmon Celery Root
        Brandade, 156
salsas
    Fresh Ice Plant, 128
    Green Coriander Seed, 113
    Tomato Marigold, 117–118
sauces see also condiments;
    dressings
    Ancho Squeeze, 93
    Broccoli Garlic Sauce, 131

Brown Butter Béarnaise Sauce,
    119
Cauliflower Cream, 139
Cilantro Cashew Pesto, 144
Green Lentil Smear, 43–44
Nuoc Cham, 152
Nutmeg Soubise, 101–102
Nutmeg Spinach Sauce, 91
Parsley Chimichurri, 84
Rosemary Maple Brown Butter,
    87
Sage, Pumpkin Seed, and Goat
    Cheese Pesto, 51–53, 143
Spiced Brown Butter Hollandaise,
    136
Tarragon Blueberry Stew, 211
Yellow Tomato Sauce, 60
seeds see caraway seeds; coriander
    seeds; cumin seeds; pumpkin
    seeds; sesame seeds
sesame seeds
    Enoki Nori Tarragon Tangle, 37
    Sesame Za'atar, 220
Shallots, Crispy, 101
Shaved Asparagus Salad, 57
shiitake mushrooms
    Shiitake Cabbage Tacos, 43–44
    Shiitake Gai Lan Noodle Bowl, 37
Skillet Cake, Winter Squash Thyme,
    215
slaws see also salads
    Celery Lovage Slaw, 76
    Chef Nghe Tran's Goi Ga, 152
    Fennel Mustard Pickle Slaw, 127
    Vietnamese Slaw, 152
Slow-Roasted Duck and Winter
    Vegetables, 186
Slow-Roasted Pork, Poblano,
    Fennel, and Tomatoes, 168
Smoked Salmon Celery Root
    Brandade, 156
soba noodles
    Shiitake Gai Lan Noodle Bowl,
        37
    Soba Noodle Bowl with
        Golden Tofu, Garden Peas,
        Cinnamon Basil, and Miso
        Carrot Broth, 63
Sorrel Hummus, 33
Soubise, Nutmeg, 101–102
soups and stews see also broths
    Beefy Vegetable Stew, 177–178
    Broccoli Clam Chowder, 160
    Corn and Smoked Salmon
        Chowder, 159
    Lentil Soup, 49–50

Potato, Leek, Mushroom, and
Chicken Skillet Stew, 167
Root Vegetable and Roast
Chicken Pan Stew, 182
Root Vegetable Chowder, 75
Sourdough Crackers, 33
Spiced Brown Butter Hollandaise,
136
Spicy Roasted Chickpeas, 51–53
spinach, baby
Baked Tomatoes, Fennel, Garlic,
and Feta, 54
Nutmeg Spinach Sauce, 91
Sprouts, Lentil, 222
squash
Basil Ratatouille, 117–118
Butternut Squash Pie, 212
Grilled Summer Squash, 114
Kabocha Squash and Ancho
Cider Broth, 51–53
Roasted Butternut Squash Steaks,
143
Slow-Roasted Duck and Winter
Vegetables, 186
Winter Squash Thyme Skillet
Cake, 215
steak: Grilled Summer Salad, 171
stews see soups and stews
strawberries
Strawberry Rhubarb Compote,
203–204
Strawberry Rhubarb Pavlova,
203–204
sumac
Sesame Za'atar, 220
Sumac Chili Oil, 33
Summer Squash, Grilled, 114
Sunchokes, Fried, 97
Sunflower Head, Honey-Roasted,
147
Sweet Corn Fritters, 211
sweet potatoes
Maple-Spiced Sweet Potato, 144
Root Vegetable Pavé, 70–72
Sweet Potato Jasmine Rice, 64
Swiss chard: Basil Ratatouille and
Swiss Chard Wraps, 117–118

T
Tacos, Shiitake Cabbage, 43–44
tahini
Grilled Eggplant Baba Ganoush,
123

Sorrel Hummus, 33
tangles
Enoki Nori Tarragon, 37
Garden, 38
Salad, 91–92
tarragon, fresh
Brown Butter Béarnaise Sauce,
119
Enoki Nori Tarragon Tangle, 37
Mushy Green Beans and
Tarragon, 106
Old-School Rhubarb, 208
Potato, Leek, Mushroom, and
Chicken Skillet Stew, 167
Tarragon Blueberry Stew, 211
Tarragon Tonnato, 151
Wilted Cabbage, 140
Tea, Vegetable, 34
thyme, fresh
Farmhouse Chicken Broth, 223
Root Vegetable Pavé, 70–72
Winter Squash Thyme Skillet
Cake, 215
tofu
Radish, Smashed Cucumber,
Tofu, and Hemp Heart Salad,
38
Soba Noodle Bowl with
Golden Tofu, Garden Peas,
Cinnamon Basil, and Miso
Carrot Broth, 63
tomatoes
Ancho Squeeze, 93
Baked Tomatoes, Fennel, Garlic,
and Feta, 54
Basil Ratatouille, 117–118
Confit Tomato, Poblano, and
Garlic, 110
Farmhouse Beef Broth, 177–178
Fresh Ice Plant Salsa, 128
Green Coriander Seed Salsa, 113
Green Jam, 43
Slow-Roasted Pork, Poblano,
Fennel, and Tomatoes, 168
Tomato Garlic Mash, 181
Tomato Lillet Splash, 193
Tomato Marigold Salsa, 117–118
Tomatoes, Nasturtiums, and
Golden Halloumi, 41
Yellow Tomato Sauce, 60
tomatoes, sun-dried: Quinoa Feta
Stuffed Bell Peppers, 60
Tonnato, Tarragon, 151

turnips
Bacon-Steamed Baby Turnips
and Greens, 155
Melted Cabbage, Turnip, and
Ham Hock, 185
Miso Turnip Purée, 171
Potato Turnip Mash, 87
Root Vegetable and Roast
Chicken Pan Stew, 182
Root Vegetable Chowder, 75
Root Vegetable Pavé, 70–72
Whole Roasted Turnip, 79

V
Vanilla Cream, Rosemary, 215
Vegetable Broth and Vegetable
Tea, 34
Vegetable Stew, Beefy, 177–178
vodka: Herb House Lemonade,
194

W
white beans: Bacon, Baked Beans,
and Kale, 164
Whole Roasted Cauliflower, 136
Whole Roasted Celery Root, 76
Whole Roasted Onions, Grilled
Garlic Scapes, and Chive
Flowers, 101–102
Whole Roasted Turnip, 79
Wilted Cabbage, 140
Winter Squash Thyme Skillet Cake,
215
Wraps, Basil Ratatouille and Swiss
Chard, 117–118

Y
Yellow Tomato Sauce, 60
yogurt
Farmhouse Yogurt, 224
Grilled Eggplant Baba Ganoush,
123
Lemon Garlic Yogurt Dressing,
171
Mint Labneh, 80
Roast Garlic Labneh, 70–71

Z
Za'atar-Spiced Eggplant Chips,
123
zucchini
Basil Ratatouille, 117–118
Grilled Zucchini, 113